On Down the Trail

Tina Knight

WinePress Publishing
MOUNTLAKE TERRACE, WA 98043

Unless otherwise indicated, all Scripture references are from the Holy Bible: King James Version.

To order additional copies of *"On Down the Trail"* send $9.95* + $2.50 for shipping and handling to:

Roscoe Knight
1100 N. Meridian #3
Newburg, OR 97132
(503) 538-4762

*Quantity discounts available.

TABLE OF CONTENTS

INTRODUCTION

"Tell us a story, Daddy."

With 640 curves in the 50 miles between our house in the Yungas, a semi-tropical area on the eastern slopes of the Andes, and La Paz, Bolivia, little people got bored, so Daddy told a story from his boyhood. As we reached the summit to start the descent into La Paz, we heard wistful sighs from the back seat.

"Boy! We won't have anything to tell our kids when we grow up."

More than 35 years have passed since Gary, Beverly and Karen asked for a story. This will sharpen their memories.

But what about seven grandchildren who will ask for a story?

We want them also to know why we went to Bolivia, what we did, and how God built His church in the Yungas.

"Write it, Tina, or it will be lost," others encouraged.

So I have written a story that began in 1955 when we, Roscoe and Tina Knight, served as missionaries for the Evangelical Friends (Quaker) church. Even though we moved from the Yungas in 1962, we've been back for visits and daily ask our Father to add other chapters to the story of the Yungas.

PROLOGUE

This is a story of the rugged Andes standing sentinel
over Yungas valleys,
of craggy mountains,
of black granite slicing into a deep blue sky,
of perpendicular, jagged cliffs,
of hazy rain-forest below a1000 foot precipice,
of clinging to harrowing one-way roads,
hugging the high mountain side,
of mudslides and zig-zag mountain trails,
of raging rivers,
suddenly turned chocolate brown;
a story of weather contrasts:
of freezing cold and steamy jungle,
of glacial whiteness covering tropical green
far below,
of sudden tropical downpours
and quiet balmy evenings.
This is a story of time-worn ritual and ceremonial traditions
played out by Aymaras,
of heroes and heroines who dared to change,
of suffering for their faith,
of "hanging on"
in the face of impossible odds,
of feast or famine,
of love and hate,
a story of Aymaras who have fought a battle
and won a victory.
This is a story of GOD, who proved Himself faithful
to lead step by step,
to protect His children,
to build His church in the Andes.
This is also the story of a family of five who fell in love
with those mountains,
valleys,
and people.
They call it *home*;
the people are *family*.

ACKNOWLEDGEMENTS

My warmest appreciation goes to my colleagues of the writer's workshop, led by Betty Hockett. Their encouragement kept me going. I'm also grateful for the assistance and counsel of Margaret Lemmons and Katie Machette who checked my grammar and spelling, then rearranged my sentences so as to make sense. And a warm hug for my loving husband for his patience, advice and counsel.

The Yungas

"Would you like to live here in the Yungas?" Roscoe asked as he reached high to pick a red hibiscus to tuck into my hair.

I shook my head. "It's beautiful, but no thank-you." Vicious little fruit flies devouring my arms took away any desire I might have had to live there.

We climbed the rocky steps to our cabin, stopping to notice the breath-taking view. Calla lilies and big blue lily of the Nile clumped along the incline, overshadowed by hibiscus bushes and *lima tomate* trees. Rocky cliffs jutted into the sky, hiding the winding road that ducked around the bend to lose itself up the canyon. White water tumbled over boulders, joining a turbulent river far below. Beyond that, dark green jungle growth covered the canyon wall. Flaming poinsettia trees lit the side of the old rock castle, which had been a vacation hide-away for a former Bolivian president.

That vacation was our first introduction to the Yungas. "Come with us. You'll love it," Samuel and Gladys Smith, missionaries from another mission, had urged. They were right. We loved it!

En route we had climbed out of the capital city, La Paz, to cross a 15,300 foot pass, where a large statue of Christ stands with arms outstretched toward the Yungas. My gaze caught the zigzag road plunging below.

Did they build that statue for a protective measure? I wondered. Little did I realize then that it would take more than a cement statue to provide protection on those roads.

In these mountains the Unduavi River is born. Starting with a trickle from soggy peat bogs, it gathers water from glaciers and springs, soon becoming a roaring giant as it tumbles over boulders, adding its bit to the headwaters of the Amazon.

Dust billowed up behind as we crept around curves and switch-backs—a narrow, rocky, one-way road following the river. Down....down....down the narrow canyon.

History had left its footprints in the rock huts and walls used as overnight inns for mule trail travelers back at the turn of the century. More recently other hardy persons had stayed there while herding their llamas and sheep along the sides of the rocky gorge.

The panorama was spectacular: a winding river, lofty jagged mountain peaks, perpendicular slate walls, snowy white glaciers suspended as from the sky, moss covered boulders half-hidden by veils of mist, water falls cascading hundreds of feet to plunge under a winding ribbon of road lost behind the mountain. Only God could paint such a beautiful picture!

With that first trip we developed a desire for regular get-aways to the Yungas for rest and relaxation. The three-hour trip down to 6000 feet provided a welcome escape from the lack of oxygen on the cold altiplano where our missionary work was centered.

Three years later in 1951 while home on furlough, I attended the yearly banquet held by the Women's Missionary Union.

"Tonight we will build a cabin for our missionaries," our mistress of ceremonies explained to more than 100 excited women. "Please roll your bills or checks to look like logs and pin them to this model of a rest cabin."

We did. With a pin carefully stuck through each rolled-up bill, we quickly built the cabin for the Yungas with $351.00.

Back in Bolivia the missionary men scouted for just the right place to build. Don Ricardo Muñoz, owner of a large hacienda, offered the ideal lot on the side of the mountain in Pichu, giving us a 50-year lease for $25.00 a year.

Roscoe and our co-worker, Ralph Chapman, marked the boundaries for the property, noting that a trail bounded it on the upper and lower sides; on the west a river flowed, while a dry wash marked the east. A tall *kayaco* tree, with large umbrella leaves, marked each corner. This parcel of land remained property of the mission for the next 20 years.

Roscoe soon found that the steep lot we leased had once been occupied. Now trees and tropical brush grew everywhere. He bought a machete and hacked out *chusi-chusi* fern, wild banana, blackberry vines, tall scraggly coffee trees and brush, leaving orange and lemon trees. Decades earlier the steep mountain side had supported rock coca terraces. Later we would use this rock as building material for the cabin.

Workmen from the mission farm at Copajira built the cabin—nothing fancy, a rustic 33 by 24-foot room with no ceiling, a red tile roof, and no plumbing. No one would call it beautiful, but it provided restful vacations.

It also provided excitement and sometimes a learning experience. A large gray field-rat, cautiously crossing the rafter, provided a perfect target for Roscoe to practice his skills with the revolver. If he didn't shoot it, the science of making a trap with a wash-tub, catching the rat, then killing it, challenged Daddy and provided excitement for the kids.

The big river below beckoned eager fishermen, while the cabin provided the perfect place for getting away from people, for reading, for sleeping and for just doing nothing! It brought joy to the missionaries, rest to tired bodies, peace to frustrated minds, and rejuvenation for those who dared to brave the roads, the insects and the lack of home comforts.

Road to Yungas over Andes

English Land Rover

Back to Bolivia

After our introduction to the Yungas we spent our furlough year in the States, then again we set out for Bolivia. With two-year old Gary on a safety leash and Beverly, a babe in arms, we traveled on an ocean freighter across the Carribean, through the Panama Canal and along the coast of South America. We had high hopes for another good term of service for the Lord, teaching at the Bible School at Copajira. Within three years our hopes were dashed.

After Karen's birth I suffered complications. For six months I fought illness including 21 days in the hospital with hepatitis. Roscoe also suffered a bout with hepatitis. We felt discouraged. Even spending time at the Yungas rest cabin didn't restore our outlook on life. We began to think about going back to the States.

"We're in a dilemma," Roscoe wrote his Dad. "We need some fatherly advice from one who has followed

7

God closely for many years. How can we know God's will for us in the future?

We have a growing feeling these last few months that our hearts aren't in the work as they should be. No doubt our physical problems contribute to our feelings, but we are wondering if we have finished our work here in Bolivia. These last three years have been hard ones. I've gained ten years' knowledge in three years' experience. It hasn't been easy. Please pray with us about this."

Six weeks later a letter from the Mission Board and a letter from Dad, both received the same day, confirmed the Lord's leading for us.

"Start packing, honey," Roscoe advised me after reading the letters. "We'll go home a year early, but we'll soon have our health back, then we'll see what the Lord has for us."

We went back to the States, bought a 28-foot mobil home, pulled it into the desert near Twenty-nine Palms, California, and spent the winter regaining our strength. Sunny days and sand provided the perfect environment for the kids to play. Shirtless and barefoot, they followed roads with their toy cars, pulled a wagon and maneuvered an old car around mesquite bushes and rocks.

"Come see what I found," Daddy called across the desert one morning. Their joy knew no bounds when they found a giant turtle, which became a favorite pet for the winter.

"Gary, watch the girls," we admonished every morning as we took our Bibles to go our separate ways into the sand dunes, sit in the shade of mesquite bushes, read and pray. During those days God spoke to us, renewing our call to missionary work. Thus, when the mission board talked to us about opening a new   field in the Yungas, we were ready.

"You will go out with joy and be led forth in peace" (Isaiah 55:12), God promised us. With renewed energy, a new call on our hearts, and a love for the Aymara people, we felt eager to get back to Bolivia.

Most adults find it exciting to get back into the work, but for little people it can be extremely frustrating. "I want to go home", Karen cried, as I kissed the skinned knee and wiped away the tears. Stumbling on cobblestone streets of La Paz didn't seem like home to her. How do you explain to a 2 1/2-year-old child that it is difficult to *go home?* The best I could do was to assure her that *home* was wherever Daddy and Mommie were. Right then, April 1955, *home* meant living from suitcases, sleeping in strange beds, traveling from the U.S. to Guatemala, then on to Bolivia—always on the move.

"Roscoe," I pleaded, "the sooner we have a home of our own, the happier our family will be. When can we move to the Yungas?" That evening Roscoe spoke to our fellow missionary, Jack Willcuts. "Let's make a trip to the Yungas this week. We want to see how things are at the cabin. We need to get settled."

"Okay. I need to visit in San Felix and Yarija. We'll have meetings each night so we'll be gone three days," Jack explained. "Let's see if Mark wants to go also, and he can take his Jeep. The old mission Jeep is in the garage as usual." He shrugged his shoulders, "Been there three weeks. No parts."

Early next morning Roscoe, Mark Roberts (another missionary colleague) and Jack Willcuts left for the Yungas. On the third morning of that trip they turned off the road to enter the private drive-way to the mission rest cabin.

"Whoa!" Mark slammed on the brakes. "Looks like we'll have to leave the Jeep here and walk down."

They hiked down a rocky, narrow road, hopping across a four-foot-deep gully.

"Apparently it has really rained here," Jack commented. "We haven't been down here for several months. Wonder how long this has been washed out?"

"It looks like we'll need a tractor to fix it before we can move," Roscoe noted.

Everything showed it had rained hard. The little river on the west had over-flowed, sending water down across the mission property, cutting deep gullies and channeling black, muddy water under the back door of the cabin.

"Look! Here's a three-foot water mark on the wall."

"Careful! Six inches of black, sticky mud cover the floor, too."

Back in La Paz when we snuggled into bed for the night, Roscoe told me about their trip.

"The mud was full of tiny biting flies. We had to sleep up on the rafters to keep away from them. The place isn't fancy and we'll have to build a road down to the house. In the three days around the Yungas road we counted over 200 mudslides. It will be hard to live down there at first. Life won't be easy."

There was a long pause. My mind skipped back to a question Roscoe had asked ten years earlier.

"Would you like to live in the Yungas?"

"It won't be easy, but with you, we'll make it fun," I promised.

I drifted off to sleep dreaming of a red hibiscus tucked in my hair.

Settling In

On May 13, 1955, six weeks after arriving back in Bolivia, the Knights moved to the Yungas. It wasn't an easy move, but excitement overshadowed the problems. Most of them anyway.

Obviously, we needed help—help in moving and help in planting churches throughout that mountainous region. Francisco had just graduated from Bible School at Copajira and felt the Lord's call to pastoral work.

"Pastor Raúl (Roscoe's name in Bolivia), I think the Lord wants us to help you in the Yungas. Do you have a place for us?"

"Come with us. I need help, and I'm sure that Tina will also be able to use your wife, Asunta, in the house. But I warn you," he added, knowing how tempting it is to seek the easiest jobs with the highest pay, "the work won't be easy."

The warning didn't discourage Francisco. Three years earlier he had asked his parents for permission to attend Bible School, but his dad had been furious about the idea.

"*My son* will never attend that school," Carlos had threatened with clenched fist raised in the air. "If you do, this isn't your home any more. You can get out!"

After more confrontations on the matter, Francisco was forced to choose. He chose to walk with the Lord.

Piling all his personal belongings in a *mantel*, a large square cloth used for carrying things, he had swung the bundle onto his back, then walked out the door. For the next three years the Bible School became his home, fellow students his family, and missionaries his parents. Now he would work with us in the Yungas.

Obviously we could not move a family of five in the little mission Jeep. We thought about it, then told Francisco, "Tomorrow we'll move. Get your things ready. We'll send everything down on a public truck."

Arriving early, the truck stopped in front of the black wrought-iron gate at the mission house in La Paz. Empty wooden crates tied to the tailgate left room for passengers with bundles and baskets, sacks of flour and sugar, and a great quantity of jerky.

"Honey, we'll never get our stuff on that truck," I fretted as Roscoe and Francisco carried out our things. Of course no one listened to me. They were involved in loading six barrels of fuel: gas for the car, white gasoline for the kitchen range, and kerosene for lamps; four beds, three trunks of dishes, pots and pans, linens, and bedding; six chairs, gasoline pressure range, a 100 pound sack of flour for bread; and other things needed to live.

"We'll see you in the Yungas," we yelled and waved as the truck pulled out with Francisco and Asunta sitting high on top.

Later that evening we arrived at Pichu to find them sitting by our belongings on the side of the main road. The truck couldn't get down to our house so they had unloaded everything up above. Thus, we had the problem of carrying everything down the mountain over a rocky, washed-out road.

"Come on, kids, let's go. Pick up something that you can carry," I ordered. But soon I realized that just getting themselves down that road was a major undertaking.

"Carry me, Mommie," Karen pleaded. As I hesitated amid suitcases, baskets of meat, fresh vegetables and fruits, and other necessities waiting to be carried, the loudest cry got my attention. Karen and I took off down the trail with Gary and Bevie, leaving the men to think of a way to bring everything down the mountain before nightfall. With little twilight in the tropics, they hurried.

The men carried larger items, furniture and trunks, between the two of them. They rolled the barrels of fuel carefully around gullies. Francisco and Asunta loaded baskets and smaller things onto their backs. No doubt they thought the *mantel* for the Aymara man and the *ahuayo* for the woman were wonderful inventions. We agreed with them.

"I'm thirsty," one child announced shortly after walking through the front door.

"Oh, no!" I groaned. I had forgotten to bring a jug of boiled water.

"I'm sure the water from the little river will be pure," Roscoe spoke with no hesitancy. "It comes out from under a big rock a long way up the mountain. It'll be safe. Let the kids drink it."

When they thought they just couldn't wait another minute for the water to boil, they drank unboiled water. It is true; a large flow of water came out from under a huge boulder. It tumbled down the mountain, flowed under the road, then plunged down our ravine. But what we didn't know was that trucks often stopped to fill radiators as they crossed that little stream. That's also where many people got off the trucks to wash their dusty faces and cool off a bit. Our pure water became contaminated before it reached our house.

In the early morning hours Beverly awakened with tummy pains and diarrhea. By mid-morning when Roscoe and Francisco went up the canyon to spend their first day evangelizing, Beverly felt no better. Her fever soon began to soar.

"Mommie, why are you standing on your head?" she asked as I gave her medication.

I knew immediately she was delirious.

"Come, we'll have Sunday School, I called to Gary and Karen. I wanted to get my mind off Bevie's fever.

"How could this happen on the first day in the Yungas?" I complained aloud.

Not wanting to frighten the children, I kept other thoughts to myself. *We're so far from a doctor. Satan's probably trying to make us discouraged and fearful before we even get started in the work here.*

After story time we prayed for Beverly.

"Jesus, please touch Bevie and make her well."

Could a child's prayer make a little sister well? I knew it could. But not until afternoon, when Daddy came home and we all prayed again, did her fever break. We praised the Lord, knowing that He had answered.

"That's our first answer to prayer in this new work," I later wrote to the folks in the States. "We will keep a list of all those answers. We've learned good lessons from this. Lesson #1: *Always* take boiled water to drink any time you leave the house for any length of time. Lesson #2: *Never* take for granted that public water is safe to drink."

Living so far from medical help could have been a fearful thing for us, but we refused to succumb to fear. We reinforced our faith in the Lord by keeping a supply of penicillin on hand. Thanks to Him, we didn't have to use it often.

Moving brings problems anytime, but during the move to the Yungas problems seemed to plague us. Standing in the midst of all the clutter that first day, I exploded to my husband, "Problem #1 was getting all this stuff down the mountain. Problem #2 was having no boiled water. Now problem #3 is that our youngest daughter needs to find a bathroom. What do you suggest?" I was tired, out of patience and out of ideas. But I picked up Karen and we went out to find some secluded spot where she could learn the delicate lessons of living in the wilds.

Roscoe, being a bit more practical, promptly sawed off the legs of a chair, making it pottie-chair height, cut a hole in the bottom, then fastened the pottie underneath. Presto! We had the perfect bathroom for little people.

A few days later after using several buckets of water that day, I cautiously mentioned problem #4.

"You have come up with some great ideas. How about tackling the water situation? I feel guilty using so much water when you have to carry it from the river, but I need water to run this household."

"You're right. I'll run a ditch off the little river to bring water down." His idea was great, but then we encountered problem #5—how to keep the water from seeping into the rocky soil.

He soon came up with another clever idea. Down the hill, below the house, he cut down a tall banana plant, then carefully peeled off the round layers. Behold! We had water pipes of banana *chala* that brought water close to the house for several weeks.

The first night in our new home no one complained about having to climb an old home-made ladder to get to our mattresses laid in the attic. It was fun and it was exciting. But after a few nights, we began to wish for stairs. Mark Roberts had built a set of stairs for their house in Puerto Perez, on the shores of Lake Titicaca, but they were too steep. Several weeks later we fell heir to them. They fit perfectly and provided hours of adventure for the kids. They proved to be my literal downfall, resulting in my using crutches for several weeks. Regardless, the stairs solved problem #6.

Another serious problem, #7, was the fact that we had no toilet facilities. Workers used the orchards or banana fields. Not having a toilet didn't bother them, but we longed to be more comfortable. We hired a neighbor to build an outdoor privy of rock. It sported a red tile roof like the house and opened out toward the canyon—with the mountain so steep, it needed no door. This tended to startle visitors, however.

It had a unique, continuous-flushing cement stool. Water from the ditch shot down the bank behind the toilet, through the stool, then underground to empty into the gully below the house. I'm sure the U.S. Department of Health wouldn't have approved, but it served the purpose and was the most romantic we've ever had.

Orchids, blue lilies of the Nile, amaryllis, orange flame vine, poinsettia and, of course, hibiscus bordered the garden path to the toilet. Tiny white jasmine vined over the roof, adding fragrance, and amidst all the flowers, butterflies flitted by day and lightening bugs every evening.

Even with all its beauty, that garden path caused little girls to race to the house at night, never daring to look back, for fear there might be "something" out there—they didn't know what.

Problem #8 involved our road—our private road. To leave the Jeep up on the main road, then walk down a rocky trail was not exactly handy. A Caterpillar tractor, cleaning slides from the main road above our private one, made matters worse by shoving dirt and rock down onto ours. Roscoe and Francisco worked long hours, even on into the night by moonlight, to clear it, but the job was too big for pick and shovel.

"Please, Lord, send a tractor our way," we prayed every day. Weeks went by with no answer.

One morning I heard a call then went out to find Don Ricardo, the owner of our property.

"*Buenos días, Señora*! This fellow says he can work on your road tomorrow, if you would like." Ricardo nodded toward a Cat skinner standing nearby.

"Fine," I responded enthusiastically. "You are an answer to prayer." He probably didn't know about prayer, but I was grateful.

Next day Don Ricardo came again to say that something had broken on the tractor so we'd have to be patient. We kept praying.

"Lord, you know all about broken tractors. Please help."

Two months passed. Finally the Cat skinner came to tell us that he could rebuild our road. We revelled in the noise of that tractor all day and thanked him profusely as he parked the Cat above the house for the night. We now had a new road and could drive down to the house.

Next morning the operator came back for the last time to tell us he had received orders from La Paz to take the Caterpillar up to the high plains, suspending all tractor work in the Yungas.

Again the Lord reminded us that He doesn't get in a hurry for the Knights, but He is never too late.

Problem #9 took longer to solve. I longed to have running water in the house. I could never have a bathroom, but running water in the kitchen seemed essential. Mauricio, our neighbor, built two water tanks up above the house. Water from the ditch ran into the first, a settling tank. This overflowed into the second one, which provided clear, clean water piped to the house.

When we built the water tanks we didn't know there would be so much speculation among the neighbors as to their use. Several months later our friend Braulio told us his reaction:

> I had a field of corn up on the mountain above your house when you came to live in Waicani (our little corner of the Yungas). On my way to the field I often paused to watch the activity down below. When the tanks were being built, I was puzzled.
>
> One evening I talked to my cousin Primo, "What do you think? What are those tanks for?"

"They're for baptizing our children so they will be Evangelicals," he explained.

I was scared.

"Stay away from those gringos," he warned.

"What do evangelicals do?" I asked.

"They teach a different religion. If we change our religion we'll get sick and the yatiri will put a curse on us. Our crops will fail, and we won't have any food," he explained.

"Ay, we don't want any more trouble than we have," I groaned.

I stayed away for a long time. But somehow I couldn't believe those water tanks were to baptize babies.

Braulio chuckled as he told Roscoe of the fear and doubt that had plagued him for many weeks.

It took several months to settle in. During this time we built a fireplace, a garage, a veranda and tackled major problems. In spite of problems and inconveniences, Waicani felt like home to us. We found friendly neighbors in near-by communities and evangelism became our number one priority.

Loaded truck on road to Yungas

Knight home in the Yungas

The Old Green Tent

"I'm worried about starting this work in the Yungas," Roscoe commented one morning after breakfast. "I'm kind o'scared."

"Why?" I asked. I had never known him to be afraid of anything.

"Mainly because I don't know how to start." He wandered over to look out the east window, down the canyon. "When we evangelized on the altiplano, we worked with Bible School students. Here, we're all alone." There was a long pause.

"Well, the Lord brought us here," he continued in a tone of voice that said 'we will accept what we cannot change'. "Surely He will show us how to do His work. It's His church."

He walked out the door to put workmen to work constructing a multiple-purpose building: garage, store-room, maid's room and guest room. Then he went off to find a secluded place to spend time with the Lord, remembering a very important lesson we learned while in the desert: *Renew your power day by day.*

Many mornings after packing a back-pack with tracts and Bible portions, Roscoe and Francisco set off to spend the day evangelizing from house to house. They would drive along the main road from one community to another but always had to hike up or down the mountain to find homes hidden among the banana, orange, coffee or jungle trees.

One morning after they left I jotted another note on our answers to prayer. At bedtime the evening before, Roscoe felt like he had the flu. I awakened in the night to feel he was hot with fever.

"Lord, if you want him to evangelize tomorrow, please touch his body and take away this fever."

Morning came and the fever was gone. Over a breakfast of hot cracked wheat cereal we talked of God touching Beverly's body. And now Roscoe's.

"I have a feeling Satan isn't pleased with our being here in the Yungas," one of us commented. "For too long this has been his territory, and he's fighting to keep it."

Later as I stood at the door, watching the pith helmet and back-pack disappear through the trees, I reminded the Lord of His promise: "As thy day, so shall thy strength be."

Next morning before the fellows left, a shy Aymara *tata* (father or respected man) timidly approached our house. Wiping the perspiration from his forehead with his sleeve, he called from the drive-way.

Roscoe went out to find an older man who talked almost no Spanish. He understood, however, that the man's son was sick and needed medicine.

At the supper table Roscoe told of his trek up the mountain.

"That little fellow has TB, I'm sure. I wish I could explain more fully to the father. I prayed for him; the Lord will have to heal."

Further into the meal Roscoe revealed his real frustration of the day.

"I just have to be able to speak to these people if I'm going to work with them," he declared. "I'm determined to learn their language."

His experience that day with the *tata* who didn't speak Spanish, prompted him to start daily Aymara study. Two years earlier he had spent three months in intensive Aymara classes, but now he dug for speaking ability, not just grammar.

Every day that first week Roscoe and Francisco visited homes up and down the valley, approaching each group they saw, whether in fields or along the road.

At the crossroads to Mina Chojlla, a group of syndicate (every farm had its syndicate) men were waiting for the Bolivian president to pass. While they waited, they gave tracts to all, then spent several minutes explaining the contents.

Mariano Surco pushed forward to get a tract. Although he could barely read, he made out the words, "*El Camino de la Salvación*", The Way of Salvation. After Roscoe drove on down the road, Mariano listened to many expressing their opinions of the tracts.

One man, more vociferous than the others, yelled, "It's a false religion. Don't read it," then promptly tore his tract to pieces, and threw it into the bushes.

"I'll take mine home to my son; he can read it then explain everything," a little Aymara lady said softly, while tucking the tract into her *bulto* along with her *chunta*, short handled hoe and freshly dug *yuca*.

Others put them in their pockets and said nothing, but two argued over the coming of the white man to bring a new religion to their community.

Mariano put his tract into his pocket and made a mental note to inquire more about this new religion.

He spoke of a Bible. I've never seen one, he thought. *I wonder what that gringo is talking about?*

The Seed, planted in the heart of this 17-year-old Aymara youth, produced a harvest in months to come.

Usually we went out into the communities to evangelize, but one evening Sebastián, a neighbor, stopped to visit. After talking a few minutes of the weather, the progress on the garage, his harvest and other chit-chat, the conversation came around to the real reason for his visit.

"I've come because I want to be a believer," the young man announced.

"Good! Let's sit over here and talk about it," Roscoe invited, as they settled themselves on a pile of building material.

"Why do you want to be a believer?"

"Last week I had a dream. I saw you in a long white robe. You were talking to me. Then someone with a big book invited me into a beautiful mansion," he explained. "I asked my neighbor about the dream and she said God was speaking to me. The next day you stopped at my house and left a little book. That's why I'm here."

Roscoe explained the way of salvation then asked, "Would you like to accept Jesus as your Savior?"

Sebastián nodded, then repeated after Roscoe a prayer of repentance. It was a happy ending to a busy day.

We closed that week with a trip to Villa Aspiasu, a village on the ridge above the canyon. While parked in the main plaza, the kids and I played Gospel Recording records to entertain the myriad village children who were always curious about blond hair on little white girls.

The men went from door to door with tracts and Gospels. All listened politely to their explanation; some had questions.

"Do you mean the Bible is true?" one woman asked. "Is what we've been told all these years a lie?"

"Please come back and tell us more," others urged.

But not everyone begged to hear the Gospel. We realized this when the Lord led us into tent evangelism.

We had sown the Word up and down the valley for two months. Now we felt it time to harvest.

Roscoe had an exciting idea. "We'll bring the big tent down from the altiplano; that will draw crowds."

"Where will you find a place large enough to pitch it?" I asked.

"The Lord will provide," he replied confidently, remembering his recent study of Abraham.

The Lord did provide—in the form of soccer fields, the only level places large enough for a big three-pole tent.

A public truck unloaded the tent, poles, and stakes, plus four evangelists—Martín, two Marianos and Báltazar with their Bibles, projector, Bible slides and pump organ—at Sacahuaya. Roscoe drove up and down the road announcing the meeting from a loudspeaker. It frightened some. They had never heard a loudspeaker before. The announcement echoed up and down the canyon, even reaching up into a logging camp across the river.

Maybe it's the judgement, the rumor spread.

Excitement and curiosity, however, brought over 200 people to the first night's meeting. Children lost their fear first and crowded into the tent to watch Martín play the pump organ. As the loudspeaker broadcast songs from the record player, adults came also. Women sat on the ground; men stood around the fringes.

When meeting started, only the missionaries and evangelists sang, but soon many were singing *"Cierta, Cierta"* (Follow, Follow, I Will Follow Jesus). After

Mariano and Báltazar each explained the Gospel story, people became restless, but quickly calmed down when Mariano lit the kerosene projector and showed slides of the creation story.

Sixty Aymaras came to Christ in those four nights of meetings. Around midnight each evening lights flickered up and down the canyon, as people followed trails back to their homes. We were thrilled with what God had done.

On Monday morning someone came to advise us that the truck we had contracted to move the tent and equipment to Arapata had gone over the bank, killing several people.

"It's too late to contract another truck," Roscoe lamented. "This is a case of making do with what we have, so we'll move the stuff ourselves."

From four a.m. until nine p.m. the fellows made two trips to move the tent, equipment, and evangelists with the trailer. On Thursday night the big green tent, pitched on the soccer field at Arapata, drew record crowds—between five and six hundred people.

................Anselmo hurried down the path to meeting. "Hurry, Marcelino," he urged his little son. "I want to get to the tent to talk to the pastors." His heart beat fast, for he knew this night he would tell everyone at meeting that he wanted to be an evangelical. He had tried to tell his neighbors of his decision but no one listened.

Tonight I will make a public confession, he thought. *It's hard for me to believe that just a few years ago I helped stone the believers in Amacari on the high plains. I didn't like them. I didn't want them to build their church building near my home, so I helped burn the roof off the pastor's house. Maybe it was my rock that broke pastor Cipriano's nose. I'm sorry. I wish I hadn't done that.* Remorse came with memories.

He stopped to wipe the perspiration from his brow on his sleeve.

Pampas grass cast long shadows in the moonlight. A *lechusa* owl flit across the path. "Aye! *kukuli* (ghost)!" He hurried, glancing behind him. He fairly flew to the circle of light cast by the kerosene lanterns in the tent. Marcelino panted to keep up with his father.

"I feel it my duty to witness to my neighbors," Anselmo testified after service. "For years I've fought the evangelicals, but tonight I want all to know that God has forgiven me."

Anselmo was one of 105 persons who prayed for salvation during the meetings. He had made his decision a few weeks earlier when *Tata* Eusebio explained that the Holy Spirit was much more powerful than evil spirits. This night, as he testified, he felt a sense of freedom from all the anger and fear he had harbored for so many years.

With the excitement of victory for the work in Arapata, we were encouraged to haul the tent and equipment to Huayrapata for meetings the following week.

We arrived on a warm October afternoon. Flies buzzed through the school room, while students recited their lessons aloud in unison, and mentally counted the days until school would be out.

Outside, women pounded their clothes on rocks, then rinsed them under the trickle of water from the bamboo tube beside the road.

"Honk! Honk!" Chickens scattered, dogs barked and mothers snatched toddlers from play in the dusty road, as our Jeep and trailer rounded the corner.

The arrival of the old green tent shattered village tranquility. The community had granted permission for a tent meeting, so a number of men snaked the tent down the trail to pitch it on the soccer field.

Curiosity disrupted the school room and soon many little boys raced down the red clay path to stand in awe as the men raised the three-pole tent. Finishing the job, Roscoe turned to the group.

"Would you boys like to have a picture?" All reached eagerly for the colored bookmarks.

"Here's one for you," he said, as he gave an orange one to Felix. "Tell your folks we are having meeting tonight. All of you be sure to come."

"*Gracias, Señor,*" came a chorus of thanks from the group.

They waited a bit, thinking there might be more papers, but soon Felix began his climb up the zig-zag path to his home hidden among banana plants and orange trees. As he climbed, he pondered the words on the orange paper.

FOLLOW ME. I wonder what that means? he thought as he tried to sound out the words.

Mama Alejandra ladled toasted pasta soup into pottery bowls, while Salustiano hungrily watched. Felix was more interested in relating all the excitement of the afternoon on the soccer field.

"It's a b-i-i-i-g tent," he measured with his arms, "and the *gringo* said that they will have a meeting tonight."

"Felix," Salustiano interrupted, "the word *gringo* doesn't show respect. Call him *caballero*."

"Yes, Papá. See what he gave me." He proudly held it up for both parents to see. "Wish I knew what the words mean. I'll ask the *caballero* tonight. Please, Papá, can we go tonight? The *caballero* said they will sing and we can learn a song and they will tell about the sacred scriptures and show some pictures too." Felix caught his breath, then raced on. "It will be a *cine*—like a movie right here in Huayrapata. Can we? Huh? Can we?"

Salustiano nodded as he drank his soup, then sucked in the fat pastas and chewed on a chicken foot.

"Yes, we'll go see what it's all about. I heard the loud-speaker announce the meeting when I was down in the coca field. I'm sure the whole community will be there."

They were—plus many from neighboring communities—300 in all. Word spread fast for no one wanted to miss the excitement.

Kerosene lanterns hung from each pole, casting shadows on the old green tent top, as Aymaras timidly gathered outside. Music from the hand-wound phonograph floated up and down the mountain. People came running from all directions. When the pump organ wheezed out the notes to "Leaning On the Everlasting Arms", the few believers began to sing and most lost their fear to crowd into the tent. Everyone was lost in rapt attention as they listened to the message that all were sinners and needed a Savior. Presently a murmur spread through sections of the tent.

"*Supayanquirinacawa!* They're devils!" someone shouted as he defiantly raised his fist and left the tent, trying to disturb the meeting.

Abruptly the lanterns began to sway and the tent bounced up and down, as the hecklers shook the tent ropes.

"*Winchincani!* They have tails," another shouted from the darkness outside.

"*Jampat mankani!* They eat frogs," a third took up the heckling.

To bring calm to the meeting, national evangelists quickly lit the kerosene projector and the group settled to watch the story of Noah and the flood. Little by little the crowd dwindled to only those who really wanted to hear the truth.

"Who would like to pray? Who would like to ask Jesus to forgive your sins and make you His child? Who would like to put your name on the list as wanting to study more about the Scriptures?"

Pedro, Salustiano, Alejandra and little Felix. That was all. Just three adults and one little six-year-old boy. But God came into the tent that night and did a work in their hearts that later changed the entire community.

The old green tent had done her duty. She was the means of starting three churches in the Yungas. We loaded her on a public truck to send back to the *altiplano*. There, after many more meetings, another fanatical mob tore her to shreds.

Tent for evangelism

Evangelizing

Challenged

Church planting for the Knights was more than tent meetings. Life also revolved around our family, fun, and those whom God sent to help us in the work.

Employees come and employees go. Francisco thought the work extremely difficult. It was. He spent countless hours hiking up and down mountain trails to pass out tracts and invite people to tent meetings. He and Roscoe spent many late hours preaching, teaching and counseling. Tent meetings required back-breaking work loading and unloading the tent, poles, stakes, boxes of Bibles and hymnals, accordion, medical kit, and other necessary equipment. In bad weather he spent time shoveling through road slides, sometimes wading rivers that had to be forded, and often walking when he preferred to ride.

When his wife, Asunta, got pregnant, they found a reason to go back to their home on the *altiplano*. We carried on alone for a time, without anyone to help us.

Raquel came to work in the kitchen but only stayed two weeks. She didn't know any of the niceties of city life. In fact, she still shampooed her hair in urine, as was custom, to kill head lice. The stench in the kitchen was just too much, and I gave her a bar of Ivory soap, then sent her out to wash her hair. When she sneaked off to spend time with workers at the river, I said, "No more," and sent her back to the altiplano.

"Lord, please send me a girl to help in the house," I prayed. "Two have come and gone so quickly. It's hard to train them, then lose them. I'll wait for your choice." I waited and He sent the right one.

Inocencia stayed with us three years. We loved her. We spent many evenings teaching her to read, using the Laubach word-picture method. Her beautiful full skirts, embroidered shawls, and derby hat made her a striking beauty. But there were times when beauty didn't prevent mix-ups.

Once when we were gone to La Paz I gave a young fellow a can of powdered milk to feed the cats and Perky, the dog. Of course he dipped into it with not too clean spoons, so after we got home I dumped the remains of that powdered milk into Perky's pan. He licked it a bit. The flies walked over it. I scraped a few leftovers from dinner on top. He ate the leftovers but left the milk below. Two days passed.

Perky isn't going to eat that and the flies love it, so we'll fix it, Inocencia reasoned. She mixed the powder with water like it was supposed to be mixed, poured it into a quart jar and put it in the refrigerator. *There, I'll give it to the dog tomorrow when he's hungry.*

We ate breakfast next morning before Inocencia came to work. I poured milk from a fruit jar into a pitcher, and we ate it on our cereal.

"Where's the dog milk?" Inocencia asked when she came to eat and wash breakfast dishes.

I gagged. Roscoe thought it a good joke. Inocencia laughed. The kids thought it hilarious. Such was life with a maid.

As I said, employees come and they go. A nice looking young fellow came to visit one afternoon then asked for our permission to marry Inocencia. We cried to see her go, but God sent us another.

At 15, Rosa had finished six years of schooling and fit into our family perfectly. She wasn't ready to think of marrying, but *was* responsible and young enough to enjoy the children.

When Francisco left, Roscoe realized it was much easier to make contacts in new communities if a Bolivian accompanied him. We tried to touch every community in our canyon with the Gospel, but sometimes we were turned down. When we made successful contacts, we held tent meetings for six or seven months of the year, starting in May, depending upon the weather.

"No," one administrator replied when Roscoe asked permission to have meetings. "The priests take care of all the spiritual needs of our people."

"No," another commented, "there's too much communist teaching around here now. We don't need any more."

"My peons need your teaching," one land owner said. Obviously, he thought the Gospel was for the poor and lower class.

Many communities, however, welcomed the meetings. Chacala was one of those. As Roscoe drove up and down the road announcing the meeting over the loudspeaker, the news reached high on the mountain to a logging camp, Moreja. After felling logs all day, loggers walked down the mountain, across the river and up the canyon to meeting each evening. Several were converted—among them, Berno.

A few weeks later, as we came home from service one evening, someone flagged us down.

"He probably wants medicine," Roscoe said as he braked to a stop.

A tall, rugged young man ran up beside the car to greet us.

"*Buenas noches,* pastor. I've been waiting a while, hoping you would come by."

"*Buenas noches, hermano* (brother). What can I do for you?" We expected to hear him ask for a Bible or hymn book, for tracts, for medicine, or for a ride out to La Paz—any number of things.

"Pastor, my name is Berno Vargas, from up on the mountain at Moreja. Since the logging camp is closing, I'm wondering if you might need someone to help in tent work. I'd like to help." Bashful, he looked down at the ground, not knowing what else to say.

Roscoe didn't recognize him. He'd been just one among many, lost in a sea of faces at tent meetings. After Roscoe had asked Berno a few questions, the Lord nudged him.

"Yes, Berno, we'll give it a try for a month and see how you like this kind of work." Thus began a working relationship that lasted for six years.

As we drove up the canyon, we talked with astonishment of how the Lord provides.

"The Lord knew just when I needed someone to help," Roscoe said. "With Francisco gone, I must have someone who loves people and who likes this kind of work. Berno does have several strikes against him. Evidently he has no education. Anyway, he said he can't read or write."

"He's just a new believer, we must remember," I reminded him.

"Yes, and he isn't married, is partially blind, and a bit bashful."

"It sounds to me like he has few possibilities for being much help to you." I didn't want to discourage him, but I really thought it wouldn't work out for the best.

Berno appeared the next morning with his few belongings tied in a pack on his back. During days of travel together, Roscoe learned his story:

"While playing in a sand lot," Berno explained, "we boys began throwing sand in each others' faces. I got it in my eye. Later my eye became bloodshot, and I couldn't see."

"Did you go to a doctor?" Roscoe asked.

"No, there wasn't any money for a doctor, but my grandmother put some home remedies in my eyes. Then my eye got worse and soon I couldn't see at all. Later I got a cataract in the other eye, so I thought I would be totally blind. Since I couldn't read or write, I worked in my uncle's butcher shop and got whatever job I could."

"You have a plastic eye now, don't you?"

Berno nodded. "When I worked for a mining official, he paid for having the cataract removed and for my plastic eye."

"Where did you learn your good Spanish?"

"In La Paz. That's where I learned to speak Aymara, too. I'm Quechua, born in Cochabamba." A truck appeared ahead on the narrow stretch of road and ended the conversation.

"Here's a man who speaks three languages and loves the Lord," Roscoe explained to me that night. "Imagine what God can do with such a fellow! One thing sure, in this case, man looks on the outward appearance but God looks on the heart."

Later Roscoe wrote his father: "Berno is certainly a man sent to us by God. At a missionary conference some time ago I listened to Dawson Trotman say that every missionary should have a Timothy. Berno is my Timothy. I want to live before him, teach him the Word and train him with God's help to be a powerful worker for the Lord. I pray I'll have wisdom and patience. It's a challenge."

Berno developed into a powerful Spirit-filled preacher, showing uncanny wisdom and intelligence. Learning to read was his biggest problem, but he had a photographic memory when it came to sermons, texts, and Bible stories. God called him and he humbly did his best to be God's man for the Yungas.

We were thankful for and challenged by the opportunity of working with those God sent us. Living in the Yungas provided a more difficult challenge. It often meant making do with what we had.

Most people think they can't get along without electricity, but we didn't have it. Every evening we filled pressure lanterns and the Aladdin lamp. We always kept candles and flashlights handy.

Doing the laundry was no small task. With no electricity and no running water, we carried water to heat on the stove, then washed clothes in a manual washer. It was good exercise for the arms as we pushed the swisher back and forth, back and forth.

One day during rainy season I hurried the process along. "Let's hang them out quickly so things will dry before afternoon."

About one p.m., a shadow passed over the house. A loud clap of thunder rumbled down the canyon. Five Knights and the maid bolted from the dinner table, racing to bring the clothes from the lines.

"Hurry," I admonished. "I hear the rain coming across Vicente's banana field." We ran with our arms loaded with clothes, barely escaping a tropical drenching.

That afternoon a Coleman gasoline iron tried my patience. It was a happy day when we got a gasoline generator so we could use a Maytag wringer washing machine and an electric iron.

With no gas stations in the Yungas, we faced the challenge of finding gas for miles and miles of travel involved in our work. We solved the problem by taking down one or two 50-gallon barrels every trip from La Paz.

We also stopped at the Camacho Market to buy two weeks supply—all our fridge would hold—of fresh fruits and vegetables. Beverly has a vivid memory of the unpleasant odor of fumes from gas barrels mixed with green onion tops. They hung over the edge of the bamboo basket, so were crushed on the gas barrel.

Arriving at home, of course, all fruits and vegetables had to be soaked in permanganate water to disinfect them—a precaution to prevent typhoid, dysentery, and amoeba.

Life could have been complicated if we had let it, but we determined not to miss what we couldn't have and to improvise where we could.

No bakery near by? We baked twice a week—loaves, dinner rolls, and cinnamon rolls.

No copper cleaner? We squeezed lemon juice and sprinkled salt on the copper bottom kettles.

No mayonnaise or blender? A rotary egg beater worked well.

Tired of semolina or oatmeal? Rosa toasted wheat in a clay pot, then ground it on the rock. Presto!—delicious cracked-wheat cereal for breakfast.

So the kids won't drink powdered milk? Try the military trick. Mix it with a little cold water, then fill the container with boiling water. After it set over night in the refrigerator, the kids thought it delicious.

Do bright shiny objects disappear? Suspect a pack rat. We found hair clips up under the rafters where Mr. Packrat had stored them.

Trouble with ants? You may have to accept them. During one vacation ants moved into the girls' bedroom, building their nest between the sheets on Karen's bed, where they laid thousands of eggs. We cleaned them out but they merely changed their nest to a straw hat on the closet shelf.

Perturbed because you buy too many rotten or fertile eggs? Try dropping them in water. The bad ones float. But the vendor may be offended, as he waits for you to prove each one sound. Listening to the maid helps you understand the situation.

"But, *hermana*, they really aren't trying to deceive you. They think a little meat is more nutritious."

Gardening presented another challenge in the Yungas.

"I wonder what's in this soil?" I questioned.

"Take some out to the farm at Copajira. Paul (a fellow missionary) has a soil testing kit," Roscoe advised. "He'll test it for you."

Next month the report came back. "You have nothing but rock." It took lots of animal fertilizer and hard work before we saw beautiful rows of radishes, onions and lettuce marching across the garden. I was so proud.

Then we made the monthly trip to La Paz and were gone three days. Returning, I stood on the veranda to view my garden. Not a sprig of green showed! Jumping off the retaining wall, I ducked under the hibiscus bush to search on my knees, but found not a trace of my garden. Only a crop of rocks lay on the ground.

"Roscoe, come," I called, close to tears. "Someone has stolen our garden. It's all gone."

A tell-tale trail told the story of the robbery. It led across the garden, down the bank, across the creek by means of a log and disappeared into the spongy mulch beneath jungle growth. *Sepes!* Cutter ants. The villains! They had neatly trimmed off every plant at ground level.

It was strange they took only our vegetables. But I was happy that they left the roses at the corner of the veranda, the orange flame vine over the playhouse, the jasmine over the toilet, wisteria hanging over the garden path and 30 orchids blooming along the terrace. We would feast on beauty and turn our attention to threatening roads.

Aymara woman

Bermo

On Down the Trail

Mudslides and Hotcakes

When we first arrived in Bolivia, the mission owned the only vehicle. Over the years some missionaries bought their own. We planned to do this while working in the Yungas. Traveling a road with so many curves demanded that we have a vehicle with good steering, good brakes, good everything.

We found it difficult to locate reliable vehicles in Bolivia. At last, we bought an English Land Rover for $1,000.00. It had bad brakes, however, so it went to the shop immediately.

"What do we do?" I moaned. "We'll have to move to the Yungas in the mission Jeep, and it's a heap."

"I agree," Roscoe nodded. "The Mission Jeep is a heap but there is no other and I'm sure it will get us to the Yungas and back." His optimism always allayed my fears. I had confidence in his mechanical ability but not in that Jeep! It did, however, get us there and back.

The repaired Land Rover, which we called "The Box", left us very uneasy on Yungas roads. One day Roscoe visited Liliana, a tungsten mine, high on the mountain above our house. As he turned off the main road to start up the zigzag trail to the mine, two portly Aymara women flagged him down, wanting a ride. Desiring to become known in our area, he consented to take them. *Then* they ran to get large crates, baskets, and bundles hidden behind bushes. These were loaded with heavy vegetables, sacks of potatoes, fruits, sugar, cooking oil, soap, etc.—market produce. Roscoe groaned when he saw all that weight.

The Box labored under its load, back and forth, up the steep, narrow, rocky switchbacks. Several times it couldn't get around the corner without backing up.

"Lord, keep these brakes holding," he prayed, as he looked down the mountain at a 60-degree angle. *Why did I pick up these women?* he worried.

Finally, forced to back up a switchback, he climbed forward on another, backward on the next, back and forth, back and forth, until he reached the top. He had maneuvered 28 switchbacks.

The trip convinced him that The Box wasn't safe for Yungas roads. We sold it for $1500.00, and bought an International Travelall.

The Travelall proved to be an almost perfect vehicle for our work. Four-wheel drive could plow through mud. It set high, so it could ford swift-flowing rivers, after someone carefully checked the river for holes, boulders, or water deeper than three feet. It was always large enough for one more. Twenty-eight adults crowded in on one occasion. We could take the back seat out so we could haul barrels of gas, tent meeting equipment, lumber and sacks of cement for building churches. We could also sleep four in the back with our youngest on the front seat.

The white Travelall proved to be so useful that we opted to take another back to Bolivia after furlough in

1960. This one was persimmon color. We drove to New Orleans, loaded it on a Grace Line 12-passenger freighter, enjoyed a ten-day trip across the Carribean, through the Panama Canal and along the west coast of South America, to disembark at Talara, Peru, just across the border from Ecuador.

Unloading the Travelall at Talara was an experience I don't want to relive. Dusk had fallen when we arrived. Talara had no dock, so we were forced to unload about two miles offshore. Wind and high ocean swells kept the ship tossing. A pilot boat and flat barge arrived just as the sun was dropping into the sea. With little twilight at the equator, darkness fell fast.

The ship's crew worked frantically to get the Travelall out of the hold before dark, but fear of denting the vehicle due to the rough sea slowed them.

A giant crane swung it out over the barge, but alas, they set it down too close to the edge. Workmen on the barge tried in vain to release the brake in order to move the Travelall closer to the center. We stood on deck, holding our breath fearing we'd see our vehicle nose off into the sea.

Roscoe put feet to his fear, ran below to ask if he could help center it. He was soon lifted aloft in a large wire basket then set down on the barge. We all breathed easier as he disengaged the brake to ease it back toward the center. Picking him up again, the crew dropped him on deck to accompany his family to shore in the pilot boat.

It would have been bad to lose the vehicle into the sea, but far worse to lose one of our children! The older ones had to synchronize their leap with the waves, as they jumped from a ladder down the side of the ship into the bobbing boat below. We threw Karen into the arms of a longshoreman, trusting he would catch her.

Darkness fell. The *Gulf Banker* bade us farewell with a toot of its whistle. As the tiny pilot boat struggled through rough seas, we felt lost in the troughs and were cheered only by pinpoints of light in the far distance as we topped the crest of waves.

After six days of travel along the desert coast of Peru, up over a 15,000 foot pass in the Andes mountains, across the altiplano and down into the Yungas, we arrived home. Changing vehicles, however, does not change road conditions. On our list of answered prayer we wrote, "Thank you, Lord, for safety as we travel Yungas roads."

Some people consider the 200 mile Yungas road to be "the worst road in the world". It is, in fact, Bolivia's version of an interstate highway. It started as an Inca trading route in pre-Columbian times and advanced to a government-built road, built with the aid of prisoners of war more than 60 years ago. In a country too poor to afford modern highways, many Bolivians travel this harrowing, single-lane highway every day to peddle their produce in La Paz. They have no other choice except to walk.

Some might think it quaint, but it's just plain dangerous. Hundreds of people have died on it. No one keeps tallies, but many crosses mark the places people plunged to their deaths hundreds of feet below. One corner is noted as the place of execution for government ministers. They were pushed into the dark abyss following a revolution.

Those who travel the road feel a need for protection by animistic gods or from God, depending upon their belief. At the summit both drivers and passengers cross themselves, and toss out their cud of coca if they are chewing. Drivers often take a drink of liquor to allay their fears of the road.

Those about to embark on the perilous journey have another protective ritual. They toss bread to the black-and-white dogs that roam the roadside. A happy, well-fed dog, the reasoning goes, sends a message to the gods: Protect this vehicle.

Past the summit where the *surazo*, the wind screaming in from the South Pole, often blows fresh snow to cover the mountains and add to the glaciers, travelers drop into an Oz-like land of lush green mountains, canyons and valleys.

Bolivian police spot-check buses and trucks piled high with bales of coca leaves used in cocaine production. The country grows coca leaves for legal consumption. Drunk in tea or chewed, coca has been a part of Bolivian culture for centuries.

Just below the coca check-point the road divides, but both the north and south Yungas roads drop into the same lush growth. Mountain bamboo, giant tree ferns, colorful begonia, Andean rhododendron, red fuchsia, and many kinds of orchids make the road a plant lover's paradise, if one dares to look.

Dipping into the dense fog of the rain forest, the road hugs the mountain side as a puny strip of dirt coursing through thousands of acres of steep, thick, sometimes cold, sometimes steamy jungle.

There are no guardrails. Clouds, obstructing the steep switchbacks, cause headlights to appear with heart-stopping suddenness through the gloom. On the other hand, the clouds' dense whiteness hide the equally heart-stopping sight of the 1000-foot precipice. Often the steady erosion caused by waterfalls creases the road with narrow crevasses. During rainy season, mudslides bury certain sections of the road. Traffic waits, sometimes for hours or days, as pick and shovel or bulldozer move debris. Traveling such roads taught us patience, caution, and that time was not very important.

During our second year in the Yungas after one especially busy week in La Paz buying supplies and attending meetings, we started on our way home. We arrived within eight miles of home, where we were stopped by the notorious Tres Marías mudslide, which cut the road in three places. Because it was Saturday afternoon, only five trucks waited to cross. Five picks and five shovels wouldn't make a dent in three mudslides, so even though we were only 30 minutes from home, we opted to make the seven- hour trip around the loop—back up to Unduavi crossroads and around through North Yungas. At 11 p.m. we fell into bed. Little did we realize this was only the beginning of our battle with Yungas roads.

Pichu mountain began to slide. It became famous the following year. Rain fell for days. Mountains became soggy. A quarter-mile-wide slide took out the road bed above our house. The crashing of giant boulders tumbling in the raging river below echoed up and down the canyon.

Forty trucks, loaded with fruit, coffee and other lowland produce, ground up the gorge or raced down from La Paz to share in commercial gain, only to be stopped by Pichu Mountain slide. An estimated 700 people milled along the road, waiting and fretting. Some helped to clean the slide away with pick or shovel, but most just sat and waited.

They ate produce from the trucks: tangerines, oranges, avocados, papayas and bananas. Rain soaked their clothes. Some slept under the truck, while others crawled under a tarp. Forty-five fortunate ones slept at the Knight house—wall to wall people across the veranda and in the garage.

Days passed. Rain continued to fall with no let up. I asked myself, *How would we feel if we were in their situa-*

tion: wet, cold, no hot meal, our fruit spoiling on those trucks? It spurred me to make hotcakes.

"Honey, do you realize that you are starting something that may get out of control? You don't have enough flour to feed 700 people."

Roscoe was right, but that evening 45 people drank a cup of hot sweet tea (four teaspoons of sugar per cup) and ate a hotcake. The next morning they got sweet coffee and another hotcake. It only helped a few, but I felt better.

"I'm going up to see what is happening at the slide," Roscoe announced almost every day. He disappeared up the muddy road, followed by Gary, who didn't want to miss out on the excitement. They came back to report progress.

"A Cat from Point-4 (U.S. aid program) cleared about a hundred yards. It got too close to the edge and went over the bank."

All felt discouraged. However, next day a Caterpillar from Mina Chojlla arrived. Roscoe came home to announce another disaster.

"A boulder came down from above, struck the track and broke it. That's two Cats out of the picture."

Slides hemmed in several trucks. Falling rocks hit some. A few drivers at the tail of the line, who had enough gas, decided to drive the loop through North Yungas. Most just waited. Dark days and more rain dampened spirits.

The report of l5 large slides between our house and La Paz left knots of fear in my stomach.

At last, after two weeks, a blare of horns announced freedom for trapped trucks. Those from below cautiously maneuvered their heavy loads up over a precariously narrow track along the mountainside, then trucks from above raced down the canyon for another load of produce.

"We're back in civilization again," I commented at supper time, breathing a sigh of relief. "I actually lived through my claustrophobia." I marveled at how the Lord had given victory over that fear.

To sit on the sidelines and watch the action from afar is one thing, but becoming involved is quite another. On one trip to La Paz we helped dig through seven slides, then waited while other truck drivers cleared five more.

Sometimes when boulders landed in the road and there was no way to move them, we built a road over the top with smaller rocks. One early morning five fellows pushed, pulled, tugged, cut, picked and shoveled until we thought we could get by.

"Get out everyone," Roscoe ordered. "Tina, guide me across." We crossed with only six inches between the tire and the drop-off. But alas, we hung-up on a big rock, had to stop, then back up, which always made for a tense time. At times like this I got a bit nervous, the kids got that frightened look in the eyes, and everyone gave too many orders.

Crossing a rockslide after nightfall isn't exactly a restful situation. One evening we arrived at the Pichu slide to find 20 trucks waiting to cross. Rocks were still falling occasionally but the tractor wasn't working. Surveying the situation, we decided we didn't want to spend the night in the Travelall and neither did we want to drive the seven hour loop trip, so we parked out of the way, locked the doors and started across on foot.

"Poor babies," we heard some mother mutter as we picked our way across the slide. More rocks began to fall when we were about half way across, which spurred our flight down the other side. As darkness fell, we slopped through mud and water another mile to reach home.

Another time when stopped by a slide we curled up in the seats to sleep while Inocencia, our maid, slept on the floor at the kids' feet. Usually the lack of comfort and the smell of squashed green onion tops from our market purchases mixed with gasoline fumes from a gas barrel persuaded us to try to cross the slide if possible. Most often we risked crossing in the Travelall. One night it was almost dark when we arrived at the end of a line of 10 vehicles.

"Why do we always arrive to cross slides when it's almost dark?" one of the kids asked.

No one bothered to answer as 11 vehicles braved the crossing. It was too dark to see falling rocks. The mud and rock gradually filled the road again, slowly oozing across to fall into the river below. But we jolted across and breathed a sigh of relief. We'd be home that night.

Others were not so fortunate. A family of four spent three days with us, then finally hired mules to take them on home. Torrential rain continued to fall. Landslides cut off all traffic. People crossed the slides on foot to walk 20 miles on to Chulumani. One day we gave a lift to a 70-year-old German woman who was also making the trip on foot.

That was a catastrophic year for travel in the Yungas. We didn't need to go far to see the effects. We pulled our lawn chairs from the veranda to sit and watch a Cat push tons of rock and dirt over the bank to land just across the gully from our house. The road crew blasted giant boulders with dynamite. Chunks of rock landed in our orange trees, while smaller pieces peppered our roof.

"Mommie, the man whistled," the children warned. All ran to open doors and windows so the concussion from the explosion wouldn't break the glass.

Thankfully, rainy seasons come to an end. But little has changed in the more than 40 years since we Knights ventured into the Yungas to plant churches. People still travel the narrow, winding roads in dangerous weather conditions, at unsafe speeds, traveling in fear and dependence upon God. Nothing has changed on the Yungas roads.

Cleaning huge Pichu slide

Over the Bank

"I'm not afraid to drive the Yungas roads," Roscoe declared, "but I *do* respect them."

The Bolivian Traffic Department set specific rules for anyone with a driver's license. One of these rules required all vehicles to receive a mechanical check twice a year. We thought it a good rule, especially for Yungas roads. Because of too many vehicles, however, and too few checking stations, some chose not to waste a day waiting in line with their vehicle. They bought the required sticker for their windshield and continued to drive with faulty brakes, loose steering, no lights, or other less serious problems.

One evening shortly after dark we cautiously crossed the Tres Marías slide to find an old, dilapidated truck creeping down a dark road. As our lights illuminated the way, the driver gained confidence, picked up speed, then pulled off at the next restaurant.

"*Gracias*," he called, as we passed. On a moonless night, traveling a narrow winding road, he had no lights!

Climbing the road to Coripata another night, we came up behind a truck worming its way along a most narrow, dangerous ribbon of road, by the light of one candle cupped in the hand of a brave fellow sitting on the right front fender. No doubt he was much more intent upon keeping that candle aglow than peering into the dark abyss below.

One Monday, a more-or-less leisurely day for us, Roscoe and the kids were down in the oranges trees, inspecting some newly built tepees. I heard screams, so ran out into the yard to look above. People stood on the bank waving frantically.

"Roscoe", I shouted at the top of my lungs. "A truck went over the bank."

My shout echoed down the canyon. He dashed up the hill, grabbed his medical kit, and we all raced up the road. The truck lay on its side in our dry gulch. Most people milled around. Some moaned. Everyone talked at once, trying to tell what had happened.

"We came around the corner," explained the chauffeur as he shrugged his shoulders and turned palms up in a typical fatalistic gesture, "but the steering didn't work so we just went over the bank."

"I saw what was happening and hollered, 'Jump! Jump!'", his assistant added, "but some didn't jump."

"I didn't want to jump without my *anafe*," a portly *chola* (higher class Aymara woman) defended herself, as she sat on the ground, dabbing at the blood on her face. "I needed that little kerosene stove. Now it's bent." She wiped her nose on her underskirt.

"I didn't jump because I wanted to find my tomatoes," another interrupted. "I dug down underneath those bundles, but I couldn't find my basket." While wrapping a not-too-white rag around a banged leg and casting a condemning eye at the offending truck, she continued, "I wanted to sell those tomatoes at the market tomorrow, but now they're squashed."

As people began to rescue their baskets and bundles from the truck, we could see that no one was seriously hurt, but we offered to help anyway.

"I'll take you up to the mine to see the doctor if you want." Roscoe said to the two injured who had ridden the truck over the bank. Of course, many then complained of having bruises, for they too, wanted to go to the mine.

That evening we walked up the road to examine the truck.

"Would you believe," Roscoe shook his head in disbelief, "both tie rods are tied on with rubber from an old inner tube. It's a wonder they didn't go over the bank a long time ago."

As we strolled back down to the house, we talked of God's care on the Yungas roads.

"Yes, He takes care of us, but He also expects us to take care of ourselves and to use good common sense," Roscoe said.

"I see a spiritual lesson in this," I added. "How many of us are searching for our basket of tomatoes or trying to find our *anafe*, precious possessions, hanging on to the things of this world, instead of letting them go and letting God take control of our lives?"

That week the chauffeur repaired the truck, or so we thought. Sunday morning we went to meeting. While we were gone he tried to drive his truck up to the main road. It had no brakes, and he had fixed the tie rods with—yes, you guessed it—another piece of rubber. When he couldn't quite make it to the top, he asked for a pull from a passing motorist. The rope snapped and with no brakes the truck careened over the bank and rolled down the mountain side through a banana field, to come to rest in a little dry creek just a stone's throw from our garage.

"The driver was thrown out," Ed, a missionary friend, explained next day. "I took him to the mine, but he died."

Word went up and down the valley that Roscoe was the one who pulled the truck and let it go down the mountain. The family tried to pin the blame on the missionary—another strike against the Gospel.

Lack of vehicle upkeep, speed, drunkenness and road conditions all contributed to accidents in the Yungas. We proved to be Good Samaritans several times.

"An excellent meeting," we all agreed one afternoon as we left Pararani with two vehicles loaded with believers. Rounding a bend on our way home, we met a Jeep neatly balanced on the edge of the cliff, with a 300-foot drop to the river below.

"It looks like you fellows are in trouble," Roscoe commented when we stopped to help.

Since the chauffeur was not able to answer intelligibly, Roscoe surmised he and five friends had been drinking and were too drunk to make the sharp curve.

"Let's both hook on to the Jeep," Roscoe suggested to Leland Hibbs after surveying the situation. "Otherwise, its weight might pull me over." Later a grateful mother welcomed her son home and thanked Roscoe profusely for taking the keys and delivering the men and Jeep safely to the door.

I learned not to expect Roscoe home when he thought to arrive. The ordinary activities of the work—discipling, doctoring, pulling teeth, encouraging the persecuted, accompanying believers to government offices to obtain justice—any number of things often caused a two-hour delay.

Sometimes there were delays beyond his control. I tried not to worry when he came home late, but night travel did make me anxious, in spite of the Lord's "Be anxious in nothing". On at least one occasion I really worried.

"When will you be back?" I asked, as the fellows loaded equipment for a trip to Caranavi early one Friday morning.

"Look for me Monday evening."

With hugs for all, we stood in the yard watching the loaded Travelall disappear around the bend up the canyon.

Time drags when we wait for a loved one long overdue. Sometimes when I stood at the window hoping for a glimpse of light down the gorge or for the familiar honk of the horn, it was a comfort to have a young son slip an arm around me, saying, "He'll be home soon, Mommie. Don't worry."

But this time Monday came and went. Tuesday came with no beep from the short wave radio. Late Tuesday evening when fellow missionaries Dave and Florence Thomas arrived from La Paz, we planned a search party. Then we heard a honk up the canyon. It was Roscoe's special honk that said, "I'm back."

"We were stuck behind a rock slide for a couple of days," Roscoe explained, while eating a bowl of soup. "Sorry the shortwave didn't reach over the mountains."

"*Así es la vida,*" the Bolivians say. Such is life in the Yungas.

Sometimes even the children worried when Daddy didn't arrive home as planned. At one evening meal, after hearing so many stories of trucks going over the bank, they cried for fear Daddy had done so.

"Don't cry. He didn't have an accident," I tried to console them.

"What's an accident?" Beverly asked.

"That's when you drink too much," Gary, the knowledgeable man of the house at that moment, explained. "You drink too much and see too many roads, so you take the wrong turn and go over the bank. Our daddy doesn't do that so we don't have to worry." That ended the conversation, took away the fear and dried the tears so we could enjoy our soup.

However, the Knights didn't go unscathed when it came to accidents. We merely had four head-on collisions. Roscoe proved to be quick enough to stop, then get his vehicle in reverse to avoid a serious accident, but sometimes not quick enough to avoid being hit. Three different times he knocked dents out of fenders and fixed headlights.

"For the man who works the Yungas, collisions are inevitable," he commented, as he wielded his rubber mallet on the dents.

Our most serious accident could have been a tragic one. Leland and Iverna Hibbs, with their two younger sons, Carol and Kenny, spent a week vacationing in the Yungas. They came down in the mission pickup, expecting to take a load of bamboo poles out to the altiplano for church roofs.

Early one morning Leland, Roscoe and Berno went down the canyon to cut bamboo along the river at Puente Villa. Hacking with machetes, in a short time they loaded the pick-up and started back up the mountain.

Approaching a sharp curve, they were surprised by a Dodge Power Wagon sliding around the corner, speeding too fast to stop. Traveling a road carved out of a cliff hundreds of feet above the river always requires courage, but it becomes extremely dangerous when challenged by a speeding Power Wagon.

CRAAASH!

The fellows sat stunned for a moment. "Wow! That was close—too close," someone said. They crawled out of the pickup to find that the winch of the Power Wagon had plowed into the radiator and water pump.

"Please, *Señor*," the chauffeur pleaded immediately. I'll pay for everything but don't report this to the traffic department."

"Where do you work?" Roscoe asked.

"I'm a traffic inspector. I also work part time for the Bolivian Health Department. Please don't report it or I might lose my job."

They surveyed the damage, spent the appropriate amount of time haggling over a fair settlement, sent the Power Wagon on its way, then discussed the situation.

"It's a miracle we weren't pushed over the cliff."

"Yeah. Replacing a radiator and water pump is a minor thing in comparison to what might have been."

The next day, after towing the vehicle to Pichu and removing the offending parts, Leland took them to La Paz for repair, then went on to the mission farm,

Copajira, leaving Iverna and Kenny to take the pickup load of bamboo to La Paz later.

Ten days passed with no encouraging word about the radiator. Each evening at six o'clock we contacted La Paz by shortwave, but there was no news of the radiator.

Just before Roscoe and Berno left for a scheduled tent meeting on Thursday, word came that the radiator would arrive on Friday.

"I'll be back tomorrow to install it, " Roscoe promised.

Next day he walked out to the main road and drove home, but the radiator didn't arrive. However, word did arrive by radio that it would be sent down the next day.

A second day he came home, then waited all day. Finally, just as he was ready to leave, a truck stopped on the main road above, dropping off a messenger with the parts.

Roscoe grabbed tools and hurriedly installed the radiator and water pump, then tried it out to see if all worked well. It did.

"Here's a *farol*," I said, handing him a little candle lantern with a small box of matches as he prepared to return to the meeting. "It's late, and you'll be on the trail in the dark.

"Bye-bye. I`ll see you Monday morning," he called as he drove up the road and on down the canyon.

"Sunday morning Iverna and Kenny left but were back within the half-hour," I wrote to the folks in the States. "On the first curve out of the drive I heard a terrible clatter but she didn't stop so I thought it was just acting normal. I heard the clatter again on the second curve and again on the third one, but still she kept going. So I went inside, planning a quiet day of rest.

Then here she came—clattering into the yard, with the fan eating into the radiator with every whirl."

"I had to come back. The radiator won't hold water," Iverna explained, as she climbed out. "Carol, get some tools and get that thing off and I'll take it to La Paz," she ordered her older son. "Kenny and I are going home."

I quickly fixed a lunch and found some head scarves and a blanket to cover them a bit to keep out the dust.

"You'll need a heavier jacket. Here, take Roscoe's sweatshirt," I offered.

We all walked up to the main road where we flagged a loaded truck. They climbed on top to find a comfortable seat among oranges, bundles and baskets, then were on their way to La Paz.

Monday morning when Roscoe came home, he found three men and a wrecked truck waiting for attention.

"*Señor*, my wife is sick and needs medicine," Anselmo said.

"Pastor, the *Señor* who is selling us land for our church building in Huancané is selling it to another because we haven't made a down payment. Please make a down payment on it," the second man pleaded.

"*Caballero*, my cousin got drunk, laid down in the road to sleep it off and a truck came along and ran over him, crushing his leg. Would you please take him out to La Paz?" the third fellow begged.

After some discussion Roscoe gave medicine for the sick wife and promised to take the drunk man to La Paz in the crippled pickup. While there, he would make the down payment on the land out of our own pocket, since the mission had no funds right then and nothing in the budget for such.

"Tuesday morning he left in the pick-up with no radiator," I continued my story to the north. "He rigged it

65

up with two barrels of water behind and a hose running from that to the motor. With the help of some baling wire, an old tin can, my garden hose and two gas barrels, they got the pickup back to La Paz. We hope this is our last accident on these roads."

For six years, day or night, we traveled the Yungas roads holding tent meetings, evangelizing, discipling and encouraging believers. Picking up dead and wounded and experiencing four head-on collisions ourselves, made us more cautious and thankful.

"I'll be glad to get off these roads," Roscoe said one day toward the end of our term. "I have probably driven more miles down here than any other white person, and only good common sense and the Lord have brought us home safe every time."

Yungas Road

The Medicine Kit

Honk! Honk! A blaring horn broke the silence. A high, shrill whistle pierced the low fog of the canyon. Going out into the yard I faintly saw someone waving up on the main road. Then he measured with his hands.

"*Cartas!*" he shouted.

Mail. Receiving mail from home was an exciting time for us during the years we lived in the Yungas. We seldom felt lonely, but isolation from our co-workers for weeks at a time kept us hungry for news.

This day Roscoe and Gary had gone across the river. Karen was sick so Beverly was playing nursemaid. And...it was raining.

I had no hankering to hike up that muddy road, but I grabbed the umbrella and set off. Receiving a big brown manila envelope containing six letters, two *Time* magazines and a *National Geographic* rewarded me for my efforts.

"Muchas gracias, Señor," I thanked the truck driver, who had so kindly stopped, then waited for me to puff up the incline.

"And thank you, Jack, for remembering us," I said aloud to no one, as the truck roared off down the road. Our co-workers, Jack and Geraldine Willcuts from La Paz, often encouraged us.

In my spare time I answered letters. It wasn't easy to write to people I didn't know, but it was a good way to make new friends. Chatting with family and friends via the typewriter paid rich rewards.

One letter went like this:

> If this letter seems a bit loud, blame it on to the kids. They are having church so loud that I can hardly think. Beverly is always the preacher. Karen is the Mama with the baby on her back. She sits on the floor in front of the preacher. Gary is the *Tata* who sits on the only seat.
>
> Beverly freely waves her arms as she preaches, whileKaren wanders in and out quite frequently, jiggling her baby up and down to keep it quiet—very true to Aymara form. Their babbling is supposed to be Aymara.
>
> At present Bevie is teaching a flannelgraph lesson using prodigal son figures, and Tata is giving a vigorous nod and a loud "sí, sí (yes)" in the appropriate pauses.

Then my letter commented on tent meetings and believers, but I soon returned to the church service:

> The kids are having an altar call now and all three are praying aloud at the same time, as the Aymaras do.

"*Vengan, no más, vengan, no más* (Come, come)," Beverly says between prayer sentences.

Now all they lack to end their authentic church service would be for one to stand, wipe his eyes, then give a long testimony. Service is over.

You asked what the kids do, so I've told you. Time out. I must put them to bed. Wish I had half their energy at the close of my day.

We found life exciting so I had no trouble finding things to write about. However, when I let that stack of mail pile up to almost a hundred letters to be answered, then I became discouraged.

"Why don't you put out a form letter?" Roscoe suggested.

"No. I'm afraid people will just drop it in the wastebasket without reading it."

But I did copy many. During those early years one read like this:

I see this letter is nothing except mumps, tumors, old broken-down cars and nerves. I'd better tell some good news.

It is pouring rain. We've just finished dinner. Rosa is baking bread.

Susie is having kittens (wanted to use my dirty clothes basket but I persuaded her that a box was okay).

Roscoe is showing off his 1,000 flea bites.

Karen is wiggling her front tooth which I'm threatening to pull if she doesn't get it out; it's only hanging by a thread.

> There. That's the latest news. Common or-
> dinary things sound funny when I put them
> on paper, don't they?

Letters revealed our attitudes so we had to be careful, lest we write about mission problems. We normally
didn't send news of illness north either—especially if it
was just a bad cold, sore throat, or diarrhea, which were
common in Bolivia. Why not write about it? Because
we didn't want our family to worry about us, and also,
because we would probably recover before they received
our letter, which usually took two weeks or more. A
few letters did show that we weren't always hale and
hearty even though we faithfully took our typhoid and
typhus shots and made a special trip out for a polio vac-
cination. The shots were a trial to the children, so much
so that Beverly fainted from fear one time. But we're
thankful they served their purpose and kept everyone
well, for the most part. Another letter read:

> Women's Bible School is history. All went
> home happy   to have been a part of it. But
> Roscoe was in bed with   fever, diarrhea and
> vomiting day and night the last three days of
> classes. He didn't respond to any medication
> that we had so I took him out to La Paz and
> left him at the American Clinic. Since we had
> to leave the kids with Rosa, I hurried back to
> the Yungas but he was back home in a few
> days. Dr. Marshal said he had paratyphoid.
> Maybe we shouldn't be surprised, since we
> drink what the brethren offer us and probably
> many times it hasn't been boiled. That's when
> we leave it in the Lord's hands. I always won-
> der about *warapo*. It's a drink made from sug-
> arcane. They just pour boiling water over

crushed, charred cane that has been tamped into a large bamboo cone and caught in a clay jug down below. The water may be boiled when it goes in, but my imagination runs wild about what's on all that cane. Anyway, Roscoe's been home three days and leaves tomorrow for Caranavi. I tried to persuade him to postpone the trip but he replied, "I promised them I'd be there so I must go." You'd never guess he had typhoid last week.

So the typhoid patient left on Friday, came home on Monday, went out to La Paz on Tuesday for an executive council meeting, on to the farm on Wednesday for a missionary council meeting, back to La Paz to buy supplies on Thursday, and came home to the Yungas on Friday to get ready for men's classes, which started on Monday. I complained of the schedule. "The work must go on," he replied. And it did. Another entry read like this:

Jan. 10—Well, here we are in La Paz. We hadn't planned on this trip but I came down with some strange bug and all the medication we had in the Yungas didn't touch it.

As you know, we are in the midst of rainy season. There is no traffic coming through South Yungas because of mudslides. We are fortunate that they are all above us so we went down to the bridge and made the circle around through Arapata and Coroico. But even between those two places we ran into trouble. About a dozen trucks ahead of us waited to cross a spongy mud bog. Fortunately, there were enough picks and shovels for them to clear it by hand, but nobody had the courage to try crossing it because they were all heavily loaded with mangos and oranges. If one of those huge trucks mired down in that bog, they'd be there until rainy season ended. There's never any tractor on that side of the mountain.

"Let the *caballero* go first," someone suggested. "If he sinks, we can lift him out." Everyone laughed, thinking that a good joke.

We weren't so sure. They might leave us sitting there all night. But we put it in 4-wheel drive and our faithful Travelall slowly ground its way across that sponge. We waved and thanked them.

Six hours later as we stopped at the traffic control on the edge of La Paz we startled the fellow at the desk.

"Where did you come from?"

"From Coroico. A dozen trucks are stranded on the other side of Ciénegas."

"What? Why, there hasn't been anyone out of the Yungas for days!" He shook his head and waved us on.

So we'll add another miracle to our list. The Lord brought us out when we had to come. We praise Him!

Our kids had their share of childhood diseases but Beverly had trouble with her tonsils. I wrote the folks:

Bevie had to have her tonsils out. They were huge, terribly infected, and we didn't want to give her more antibiotics. Doctor said to take them out.

We gave her vitamin K for a month but her blood wouldn't coagulate. Her tonsils were so infected, the doctor thought it better not to put her to sleep. So she just sat in a chair as an adult, received a local on each side and out they came. She succeeded in splattering blood all over the doctor, but he didn't seem to mind. "She's braver than most adults I've attended," he said.

I'm writing this at the Clinic. Bevie and Roscoe just came out of the operating room and the nurses said, "*Ella es muy valiente, muy valiente,* (She's very brave, very brave)." We're proud of our little 11-year-old daughter.

Since it was often a month between times we received and sent mail, I usually put off writing until the last minute, then worked hard to meet a deadline. Late at night, propped up in bed with a typewriter on my lap, I wrote while waiting for Roscoe to come home from a meeting. But the reward of receiving mail was high pay for the time I spent at the typewriter.

Dreaming of clever ideas for articles to be published in the States was a challenging assignment, but not always easy. One was entitled "The Medicine Kit":

"That kit definitely needs a new coat of paint," I heard the *Señora* say one morning. "Any doctor in the U.S. would be ashamed to be seen carrying one like that." But the man of the house, without giving my condition another thought, carefully picked me up and went off to treat another patient.

Yes, my body is an old metal fishing tackle box, and I'm filled with bottles of pills, ointments, syringes, tooth extractors, etc. I'm battered and scarred with many years of use, but age doesn't impair my usefulness.

I'm not proud, but I would venture to say I'm more in demand than any other piece of equipment in the work of the Yungas. The car never leaves the yard without me and sometimes I go on muleback or am carried by hand up a mountain trail.

I'm a bit heavy, but believers offer to carry me, happily thinking of the aspirin or shots which await them after church service. It's strange, but many plead for my shots instead of my pills, for they reason that the more the remedy hurts, the better it is. I carry several kinds of injections, but the vitamin is far more popular because it burns so much.

I have made some enemies; babies cry and little children hide behind their mama's skirts when they see me coming, but I have made many more friends. Some have been converted to Jesus because of me. There have been very few whom I haven't been able to help; most go happily back to their homes with aspirin, worm pills, yeast tablets, sulfas and the shot.

An interesting sideline has been the conversations I've heard.

"*Señor*, will you come up to my house? My little brother is sick." I was soon off on another errand of mercy. The hut was damp and dark but within moments our eyes focused on the still small form of a 6-year-old boy, lying on a hard pallet in the corner. We could find no pulse; his limbs had grown cold;

doubt was written across my owner's face. We were probably too late. Hadn't they told us that the witchdoctor had been there with his incantations and high prices?

Leaving pills, the inevitable shot, and a prayer, we left the hut, with little hope of seeing the boy alive again.

A few days later we stopped by to find our patient almost well and on a table by the bed lay the Bible we had left.

"Thank you, Lord," my owner prayed as we ducked under low eaves then wound our way down the path to the car.

"*Señor*, will you pull my tooth? I can't sleep at night because it is full of worms."

Out came my forceps to pull a rotten tooth— and without procaine. Many in this Yungas valley think every cavity is caused by a tiny worm.

"I need some medicine, *Señor*. I've been eating too many bananas." I gave them some pills, smiling, because they think those tiny black seeds in bananas cause intestinal parasites.

"*Señor*, I whacked it with a machete," a teenage youngster explained as he held up a blood-soaked hand with one finger dangling. I provided sulfa powder. My master carefully taped it to a tongue depressor. I heard him tell the young fellow to come back that afternoon. We planned a trip to see the doctor at the mine. But he didn't come. Several weeks later we saw him along the road.

"Andrés, how's your finger? You didn't come back to go with me to the...."

Before my master could finish his sentence, Andrés held up his finger, wiggling it vigorously. Evidently my medicine works.

"*Buenos días, Señor*! I've walked five hours down the   mountain to your house because I hurt. Will you listen to   my heart with your machine?"

"Where do you hurt?"

"Down here. My heart hurts down here," the old woman said, as she touched her abdomen.

"And where do you hurt?" he asked a young girl later.

"My arm. My mother-in-law put a curse on me and my arm hurts," explained the new bride.

"And you?"

"My eyes, pastor, I can't see. I fall down when I walk along the trail and I can't work as I used to. I want   medicine for my eyes," the aged grandmother pleaded.

"And you, *Tata*? What's your trouble?"

"And you, Mama?"

"And you...?"

Sometimes the missionary is tempted to leave me at home, for I cause him so much time and work, but then he   thinks of the needs: the *mamas* and *tatas*, the old and the young, the believer and the non-believer.

Again my bottles are refilled, needles for syringes are boiled, and I'm packed, ready for another trip for the Lord.

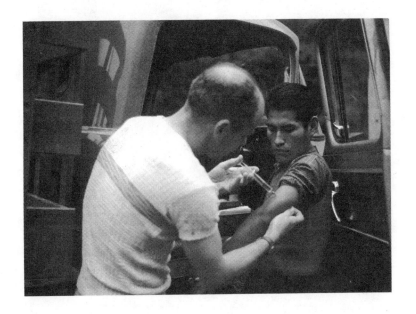

Roscoe giving injection

On Down the Trail

Fun

"A real playhouse? Not just a quilt thrown over chairs in the living-room?"

The girls were skeptical, then thrilled to hear Daddy say, "Yes, a real playhouse."

Living in a small house made it necessary for Gary, Beverly and Karen to play outside sometimes. But, living in a two-season area—rainy and dry—dictated their choices for play.

We solved the problem of play during rainy season by building a playhouse. Built of rock and sporting a red tile roof, it made a delightful play area.

"Mama" Beverly kept the house, ground chile on the rock, washed coffee beans, laid them out to dry, and prepared meals for the family. Karen cared for the baby in the doll buggy and ran errands for "Mama". "*Tata*" Gary went hunting and arrived back home for meals. Their play usually depicted the lives of the Aymaras. When they tired of playing in the playhouse, their studies provided other ideas for play.

"Where are you going today, Daddy?" someone asked almost every morning. One day they heard him say he would be home, so immediately they grabbed his hands to lead him down to their tepees. I followed.

We picked our way down a steep path, bending over to keep our heads out of the brush. We waded through a bit of mud and stumbled over some hidden roots. Then we crossed a fast-flowing little creek on some rather precarious rocks, to finally arrive at their favorite haunt for the moment.

Here the Indians, either Apache or Shawnee, depending on their choice for the day, lived, cooked over a make-believe fire, fished in the stream for imaginary fish, ate oranges and green bananas and brought their water from the stream through a banana-chala trough.

Roscoe exclaimed properly over their home in the woods. I was more practical.

"You don't drink the water, do you?" I asked.

"No," Gary answered.

There was a pause.

"No," Beverly echoed.

"No," parroted Karen, while busy with the baby on her back.

I'm still not sure they told the truth that day, but their knowledge of living off the land, as the American Indians did, proved to me they had profited from their studies.

Every year we received Christmas and birthday money from friends and relatives in the States.

"What shall we do with our birthday money this year?" someone asked after helping Bevie celebrate another year on a hot summer day in January.

"Build a swimming pool," Gary promptly suggested.

"Yea! Yea!" the girls agreed loudly.

We all thought it a great idea, and built a swimming pool for $53.00. It was just a small 10 by 20-foot one, ranging from two to six feet in depth, but big and deep enough to provide lots of fun for the kids and relaxation for us who seldom took time to relax.

However, it also proved to be dangerous. When Gary rescued the girls after they tipped off an inner tube in deep water, rule #1 became very important: *Everyone had to learn to swim.*

Nevertheless, we could not control all who came to visit. One visitor, missionary kid Greg Clarkson, tripped to fall into the shallow end of the pool. He just lay there. Evidently the fall knocked the wind out of him. Fortunately, Gary was there to pull him out. Another time missionary kid James Roberts took his turn falling in. Again Gary came to the rescue. We learned to watch visitors closely, lest we lose one in the pool.

For the most part, however, the pool provided many hours of fun for our family. It was birthday money well spent.

Camacho market is noted for selling many things, but I hardly expected to buy a dog there. As we picked our way past Aymara women with their wares spread out before them—avocados, tomatos, papaya, *yuca*, eggs, balls of hardened cane syrup wrapped in banana leaves, and other market produce—my eye spotted the birds so I stopped to look. Black and yellow canaries trilled their morning song. Multi-colored parakeets chattered to their mates. Myna birds whistled, green Amazon parrots stared with their red eyes, and a giant brilliantly colored macaw watched as we admired him.

A little brown face with knitted *gorro* pulled low over its forehead peeked from behind a pile of merchandise.

"Please, lady, would you like to buy a pair of *abarcas*? I'll give you a good price." The boy held out a pair of rubber-tire sandals.

"No, thank-you." I wiggled my forefinger and pressed through the crowd to catch the family. *Everyone pressures to sell something—dogs, abarcas, candles—it would be nice just to look sometimes*, I thought grumpily, forgetting that they were trying to make a living. Then a man offered us a pup.

"Can we keep him, Daddy? Can we keep him?" With three kids jumping up and down, all clamoring for the dog, how could he deny them this little ball of black-and-white fur?

"Yes, we'll take him." He handed the man a coin.

"Who will hold the pup?" was the main argument, as we savored our lunch of *salteñas (a spicy meat pie)* while bouncing along the Yungas road on our way home.

The pup won the argument, for he didn't want to be held. As he jumped up to look out the window, his black-tipped ears perked at an inquisitive angle prompted his name.

"Let's call him Perky."

And so it was that a little black-and-white Heinz variety dog with perky ears became the beloved pet at the Knight house. He was the first of a long list of pets to be loved and cared for.

About the time Perky came to live with us, someone gave us two kittens, Susie and Sammy. The girls were thrilled, for the kittens would ride in the doll blankets on their backs, something that Perky would never consent to.

Susie was a fussy little lady. She insisted on having the best for the birthing of every family.

"Mommie, come quick! Susie's having her babies on my bed," Gary hollered down the stairs. I ran to carry her to a prepared box. Another time she wanted to use the laundry hamper. But the most exciting time for the girls was when they found Susie with six little calico and gold kittens sleeping contentedly in the doll buggy in the playhouse. Real live babies in their doll buggy!

Of course we didn't want to get overrun with cats so had to get rid of them. This was always hard for the girls, but at one pastor's conference the kids became typical Bolivian merchants.

"Anyone want to buy rubber for a *flecha*?" Gary asked the men as they came to buy sugar for their coffee or pasta and rice for their soup. Cutting off strips of inner-tube for slingshots and selling them piece by piece proved to be a good business.

The girls were not about to be outdone, so they put the kittens in full view.

"Please give me a kitten," several pastors begged.

"You can have one if you will take good care of it."

Thus they gave away all the kittens. But invariably six months later some came back asking for more kittens.

"What happened to the one we gave you?"

"It just died, *por sí no más* (of its own accord)," they replied. Of course everyone knew that cats made good eating in some households in the Yungas, and the men had a hard time convincing the girls.

Finally Daddy stepped into the picture. One morning when he thought the girls weren't watching, he took some new kittens—that prolific Susie!—to get rid of them but the girls saw him. Then came tears. How do you explain to little girls that we can't be overrun with cats?

The list of household pets grew from the usual to more exotic ones. Little green water turtles made the trip from New Orleans to Peru on the ship, *Gulf Banker*, then rode several hundred miles over the Andes to be at home on the veranda in the Yungas.

"Mommie, come quick! Lady's eating our turtles," Karen cried one day. Lady, our lovely collie dog, who was merely satisfying her curiosity, had bitten through their shells and of course they died.

Karen loved insects, but one of her pets, a large tropical beetle, was not well received.

"Inocencia, see my bug." She proudly held her prized pet for the maid to see.

"Aye!" Inocencia screamed. "Get that thing out of here. It'll bite you." She swatted Karen's hand, sending the beetle flying through the air, to be lost in some dark corner. Karen was crushed and went to bed sobbing. Next morning we saw the   pet beetle disappearing out the door to safety.

Gary's hunting trips also provided pets. After one vacation he brought home a small green Amazon parrot, with yellow wing tips and bright red circling its eyes.

Polly was fussy about what she ate but not at all too fussy about her table manners. Her corner of the veranda was always a mess.

All our efforts to teach her to talk were to no avail. Polly would only chatter that special parrot talk. Large flocks of parrots flew over the house, chattering as they passed and Polly always had the urge to fly away with them, but Gary had clipped her wings. Upon hearing calls from her kith and kin, sometimes she flew off her perch, but landed down below in the blooming impatiens. Red and green parrot mixed with red and green impatiens, often caused us to think that Polly had flown away for good.

"White mice!" I exclaimed with horror when Gary suggested them. "Where did you get the idea of having white mice for pets?"

"I read about them in the *World Book*," he answered, "and remember, we had that science lesson in school."

At that moment I could have denied having studied anything about white mice, but decided I'd better go along with the idea.

"Daddy, will you help me build a cage? Mommie says I can get some white mice, but I need some place to keep them."

"Mommie said you could do what?" Roscoe's hand poised in midair, as he started to bite into one of Rosa's cinnamon rolls.

Seeing my reputation as a kind, loving mommie was at stake, I hurried to explain.

"Yes, they can have white mice, but I insist they keep the cage on the veranda and not in the house."

It was a happy day for all three kids when they went to the American Clinic in La Paz to buy two white mice— —supposedly a "mommie" and a "daddy".

We were surprised at how much information one can glean from the *World Book* on white mice, as our young son knew all about kinds of food, housing material, and everything necessary for raising healthy mice. All went well with the project for the first week or so.

"What's that terrible smell?" I exclaimed, more to myself than to anyone else, as I lay back into the swayback lawn chair on the veranda. Then it hit me—the mice!

"You'll have to get rid of those mice."

"No," they begged. "We'll clean out the cage."

They did for a few weeks. Enough time for tiny blind, hairless babies to be born. Susie and Sammy often sat watching the mice activity and probably dreamed of a delicious mouse dinner. Soon they realized the fulfillment of their dreams and that ended the saga of white mice.

After Perky and Lady went on to dog heaven, Cinders, a black purebred cocker spaniel, became our watch dog. But he met a sad fate. A jaguar came up our canyon, killing livestock and other smaller animals. One night Berno heard Cinders race down the path barking furiously. Then he heard "Yip-yip-yip-yip". We heard no more from our beloved Cinders. Evidently the jaguar carried him off for a meal.

Of all the pets we owned, rabbits proved to be the most lucrative. With Daddy supplying funds for rabbit pens, five does and two bucks—big beautiful New Zealand whites—the kids were in business.

This venture taught valuable lessons for years to come:

......keep the pens tight so bats can't feast on rabbit ears.

......it takes hard work to pick feed for as many as 60 rabbits.

......if you don't feed them, they die.

......there are always a few that don't make it to adulthood.

The kids learned other good lessons too—about death, the value of money, how to tithe, responsibility, and how little by little you can save to have quite a sizeable sum.

Pets were so much a part of our everyday life that the kids even held funerals for those that died. The first pet buried in the pet cemetery up by the water tank was a wild canary, which was placed in a small match box.

Probably the saddest funeral was that of a pet rabbit. Beverly gave special care and tidbits to Peewee, the runt of a litter. When he died they found a small shoe box, and carried it up the drive-way to the cemetery. The three of them sang "When The Roll Is Called Up Yonder", Gary preached, and Beverly prayed. Karen cried and Gary covered their pet with dirt to leave him to go on his way to rabbit heaven. Life was a serious thing at that age, and death was hard for the owners of much-loved pets.

When we arrived to live in the Yungas, Gary found it a hunters' paradise for those wielding slingshots. We often awakened to find Gary and Karen gone, their beds empty.

"Karen," Gary whispered in her ear. "Come on. It's time to go." Quickly they donned jeans, tee shirts, and tennis shoes, to sneak out into the cool morning. Clutching a slingshot, they crept down the narrow, rocky path to the orange grove.

The *uchi*, from the oriole family, builds its nest in the high trees overhanging the river or above a steep cliff. It swings from an intricate weaving of straw, safely protected from snakes. Many an uchi breakfast was cut short by a 10-year-old hunter, trailed by a hero-worshipping five-year-old sister.

Gary soon graduated from stalking birds with a slingshot, to a BB gun, later a pellet gun, and finally to Roscoe's .22 caliber rifle. It was a thrilling experience when he brought home a sari, a large rodent looking much like a wild pig.

"Where did you find it?" Roscoe asked.

"Across the river in the orange grove. Probably headed for Lorenzo's yuca field."

We're sure Lorenzo was pleased, for several saris found their way to the Knight's dinner table, thanks to a son who was becoming a good marksman.

Living on the river should have provided many fun times of fishing, but somehow we were always too busy except when we were reminded.

"Remember, Daddy, you promised." This reminder produced short trips close to home. But the famous trip was to the Altiplano.

It was a sunny day in La Paz. We loaded fellow missionary Marshal Cavit's little fishing boat on to our Travelall and left for Jichacota, a crystal clear lake at the foot of an Andean glacier. Wind began to blow as we got closer to the lake. We pulled our coats close, in spite of the sunny day.

The menfolk launched *Corky*, a little ten-foot boat that lived up to its name. Roscoe carefully helped each of us into the bobbing boat, with firm instructions to sit still, so as not to tip the boat.

Stepping into the water with his hip boots on, he planned to push out a bit from shore before jumping in, but alas, the shore line dropped sharply. We screamed and the girls cried, for the family almost tipped into the frigid water.

"Let's go home," someone pleaded through chattering teeth.

"Not yet," Roscoe tried to encourage us. "Let's sit still so *Corky* won't dump us and we'll putt around the lake a few times to see what we can catch."

But neither the beauty of the lake, mountains and glacier, nor catching ten nice lake trout could reactivate our enthusiasm for fishing that day. We took pictures of three freezing little fishermen with their days' catch and entitled it "the end of a miserable day at Lake Jichacota, 14,000 ft. in the Andes."

Even though our children loved going to the altiplano to play with other missionary kids, nothing quite compared with the recreation of the Yungas. Other missionary kids [MKs] came to enjoy it also. Stuart Willcuts came for a visit in March, when rainy season was almost over and a Caterpillar tractor was repairing the main roads, which had been left in sad condition because of rockslides.

"Remember, kids," Roscoe warned, "if you hear the tractor working up on the road, don't play down in the orange trees, for they are pushing a lot of rock over the cliff above."

"Okay."

It was a warm afternoon. Doors and windows stood open. All was quiet. Karen napped upstairs while the three older ones disappeared somewhere to play. I heard the roar of the Caterpillar but thought nothing of it, for it often worked up above. Dirt and rock shoved off the road came tumbling through the jungle growth below.

In a few short minutes, the kids raced in to flop on the rug, white as ghosts.

"What's the matter?"

They all tried to explain at once.

"Wait a minute. Don't all talk at once," I tried to calm them. "Now, tell me what happened."

"We went down to hunt birds." Gary's voice trembled. "We were creeping along real quiet, so as not to scare 'em, when all of a sudden, I heard rocks tumbling through the trees. Then I heard the tractor and thought of what Daddy said. So I grabbed Bevie's hand and Stuart grabbed the other one and we raced up the hill. We hadn't gone very far when we heard a really big rock come down the mountain."

After supper we all went down to find a boulder the size of a Volkswagen bug in the orange trees. It bounced across the trail only seconds after the kids raced up the path to the house.

Later that evening after the kids had gone to bed, Roscoe and I stood in the yard gazing up at the stars, then down into the dark canyon below. We listened to the roar of the river, the tree frog whistling from the palm tree near the pool, the chirping of a cricket hidden in the giant split-leaf philodendron near the corner of the veranda, and the shrill buzzing of the cicada from the hibiscus bush. Over all the sounds, fireflies flitted through flower beds and along the garden path. It all reminded us that whether we were at work, play, or in the midst of danger, God kept His hand over our little corner of His world. We were thankful and reminded Him that there were others up and down the canyon who also needed His care.

Beverly & Karen

Gary with a sari

On Down the Trail

A Faithful Witness

Segundina, tall, barefoot, and wearing the typical full skirt and derby hat of the Aymara woman, trotted down the path.

"*Buenos días, hermana*," she called from the end of the veranda.

We sat to visit—she on the cement floor as she was accustomed to and I in a lawn chair. That first year in the Yungas I often sat there to watch the view below. It was a restful scene—a steep mountainside covered with jungle trees and vines, an old sawmill in a small orange grove nestled at the foot of the mountain, and a swinging footbridge, minus several boards, precariously spanning a roaring river.

Uchis and *quehuays* landed in the orange trees near the creek. As Mama Segundina seated herself, I heard the "crack" of a slingshot used to scare the birds away. Evidently our neighbor Juanito was nearby, carefully guarding his fruit.

"*Hermanita*" (sister in the Lord). She drew out the last syllable to an endearing pitch. "I've come to visit and I've brought you a gift." She handed me a small bundle from her *ahuayo*, that grey and red striped blanket that she used to carry things on her back.

I opened it to find eggs snuggled in a nest of dried coffee beans, her thank offering for our coming to the Yungas.

"I'm glad you've moved to Waicani. I've talked to all my neighbors about Jesus but they won't listen. They say I'm crazy. Now you can help me win them to the Lord."

"We will, Segundina. Tell me your story. How did you find the Lord?" I asked.

She told a long detailed story, concluding with a passionate summary of her quest for peace.

"I searched for God for a long time and at last I've found Him. I don't know what makes me feel different, but I do." She laid a work-worn hand over her heart. "I prayed and found peace and rest. For years I visited churches, burned candles before the saints, climbed on my knees to *calvarios* high on hill tops, spent time and money and tears searching." Her voice trembled. She sniffed and wiped her eyes. "At last I've found what I needed. I found Jesus."

"Yes, we'll help you win your neighbors, Segundina."

This precious saint had faithfully sown the Seed, but now someone needed to harvest.

"The success of the Old Green Tent proved that tent evangelism is the way to go," Roscoe said after hearing Segundina's story. "I have an idea. The mission has a little 16 by 16-foot army tent in La Paz."

"You mean the one that South Salem church sent down a long time ago?" I interrupted.

"Uh-huh."

"But it's too small," I argued.

"Well," Roscoe shrugged his shoulders, "it's all we have, so we'll use it."

The entire community of Pichu, more than a 100 people, crowded into the little patched one-pole tent. The kerosene lantern hung from the center pole providing light but also attracted myriad insects. Music echoed up and down the canyon, calling people to the meeting. They all came, old and young, excited and curious about these special meetings.

Ducking under the tent flaps, held high on tall poles, men removed their hats to stand far in the back. Women ventured closer to the front, sitting on the ground. Two benches beckoned the most courageous. Tired mothers, arriving from a long day in the fields, jiggled fussing babies. Dogs and kids wandered in and out, but for the most part, all gave rapt attention when the service began.

Arriving late, Genoveva hobbled down to the front. "*Buenas noches*," she greeted her neighbors, as she removed her derby hat and timidly sat beside Segundina.

I played the accordion to teach them simple choruses. Then all was quiet as Francisco, using a large picture roll, explained the story of the Prodigal Son.

Afterwards, Roscoe emphasized the importance of the Scripture.

"The Holy Scriptures, the Bible, is Truth." He held his Bible high to explain the way of salvation. "It says, 'All have sinned and come short...'"

Segundina stood to boldly exhort her neighbors to come to her Lord to find peace.

The final night was a joyous one when 15 people knelt to confess their sins. Lorenzo watched as Alejo and Manuela walked to the front. Then Anselmo and Rosa. Augusto and Norma. He felt uncomfortable, shifting from one foot to the other and back again. Then, as if pushed by an invisible hand, he made his way through the crowd to the front. Glancing sideways at his wife, he nodded with his up-tilted chin. Genoveva picked up her bent stick, then hobbled to stand beside her husband in front of the missionary.

"Let's pray," Roscoe said. "I'll pray, you repeat after me."

As he prayed slowly, the crowd repeated phrase by phrase. Some prayed along with the group so as not to be different. Others meant it with all their hearts. Tears fell in the dust, showing their sincere intentions. No one was more in earnest than Genoveva. She had watched Segundina's life and wanted the same peace and joy.

"Lord Jesus, I accept you as my only Savior...." As the missionary laid his hand on her head while praying, she felt a tingle go through her body. Her prayer mixed with tears of repentance, joy and true thankfulness.

With cooperation from the weather, the little one-pole army tent served well for meetings throughout the valley. A public- address system hooked to our car battery, carried the message up and down the mountain. Excitement and curiosity ran high. But opposition also raised it's ugly head.

We pitched the tent at Chaco, in the shadow of the old rock castle surrounded by flaming red poinsettia trees with a background of a tumbling white-water river. Many came to listen. Some stood on the outside, however, making fun of those who had courage to step inside the tent.

"Aye...aye...aye-aye." Drunks sang to disturb the meeting, then pulled up tent stakes and let one corner of the tent down on someone's head. A fight started between a woman who wanted to listen and some who didn't. At that moment a clap of thunder rumbled down the mountain, announcing rain, which promptly broke up the ruckus.

"Please come back for meetings." Juan Pati spoke for 20 new converts. "Come until we know our Bibles well enough so we can lead our own services."

To assure himself that we would keep our promise, Juan appeared at our door the following week. We visited. We talked of road slides, of the weather, of sari eating their crops and other mundane topics.

"Pastor, may I have some leaves off your orange tree?" Juan finally asked timidly, glancing up into the tree above our heads.

"Sure. Take all you want. But I'm curious. What do you use sour orange leaves for?"

"For medicine. It's good medicine." Careful to leave what the cutter ants had nibbled on, he proceeded to pick a couple of handsful of leaves and placed them in a small square of cloth that he pulled from his pocket.

"How do you use it as a medicine, Juan?" I inquired. I could not imagine the leaves being good for anything, since the fruit was so bitter and sour.

"*Hermana*, just put the leaves in a *tina* (wash basin), pour hot water over them and when it is cool, put your feet in the water and it will cure your headache," he explained.

"Uh-huh," I nodded doubtfully, wondering about the effectiveness of the process.

Clutching his prized medicine, Juan went up the road with a reassuring promise that we'd be there that night for meeting.

The following week we took the tent to Yarija for meetings. To get there, we had to leave the car by the side of the road, then walk a half-hour up the mountain. Men and mules carried the equipment, but we walked—all five of us, single-file, up the trail.

It was hot. We were thankful for our pith helmets but longed for a drink of pure water. For a three-year-old it was a long, hard climb, so Karen and I took our time, stopping to pick tangerines to quench our thirst—a permissible custom in the Yungas.

That evening we set up housekeeping in the tent on the soccer field. A believer had received permission to hold meetings so we settled in for three days and nights. Ants and fleas nibbled on us at night. During the day the wind blew sand under the tent curtains until everything tasted gritty and we felt grimy. With little water for washing, we endured it and called it a picnic.

The curious poked their heads through the tent flap in the morning before we could get out of our sleeping bags. Since their day starts early, Aymaras see no reason for sleeping after the rooster crows somewhere around five o'clock. One old *Tata* wandered in to squat on his haunches and talk, until we cautiously mentioned that we needed to get up. I'm sure he wondered why we didn't just get out of those sleeping bags. Why all the concern about privacy when everyone sleeps in their clothes?

The Aymara cannot understand the Westerner's desire for privacy. Dishonest and evil deeds need to be kept out of sight, of course, but why anything else? What do you contemplate doing that the public should not view?

For breakfast *Tata* Nícolas brought hard rolls and

porcelain mugs of *sultana*, a Yungas drink made from toasted coffee husks. With four teaspoons of sugar and lots of milk, it was delicious.

Nícolas, a happy believer, loved to make others happy. Gold teeth flashed in his smile as he told his story:

"I lost my hand at a *fiesta*. I thought I knew how to handle dynamite but something happened and it blew up before I could let go of it." He held up a stub for us to see, then chuckled. "I've learned to work with one hand and a stub."

"Life hasn't been easy," he continued. "One by one, my children have died. Only a daughter remains but she works against me, saying I'm a `fanatical evangelical'". There was a long pause. "Maybe I am," he continued. "My life was changed when I met Jesus and that made me fanatical for the Lord. I won't have long to live. The doctor says I have TB. But I want to preach and win my neighbors until He calls me home."

Another long pause..... "Since I know that I don't have long to live, I bought a casket in La Paz. I brought it down on the truck. I keep it in my house and loan it to anyone who wants to borrow it. Several have used it.

"'I don't mind you using it,' I tell them, 'but be sure to get it back by the time I need it.'"

When Nícolas finished his story, he picked up our empty mugs, said "*provecho* (may your breakfast profit you well)," and bowed out of the tent as we all called "*muchas gracias*".

"What a delightful view of death," we commented afterwards. "He isn't afraid of it, just wants to be ready. He also wants his neighbors to be ready."

Later we had another host for the evening meal. "Dinner's ready," *Tata* Pedro announced as he peeked through the tent flap. Four o'clock dinner was company fare.

Crowded around a small low table, we savored a two-course meal. The first, fried pasta soup, made with *ají*, spicy red jalapenos, had pieces of fried potato floating on top. Beverly thought it too hot, but the others enjoyed it. The second plate was more appetizing yet— fried rice, boiled bananas, boiled potatoes topped with a fried egg and a piece of fried jerky. Delicious!

Again that evening the devil fought our efforts in evangelism. The leader of the opposition rallied his supporters for a meeting on the soccer field where we had pitched our tent. "Don't listen," he advised. "They are communists preaching a false doctrine."

We received two notes from the secretary of the local syndicate telling us to leave. In spite of the opposition, however, eight new converts were added to the church. Sometimes the children and I stayed at home to do school work but tent meetings were exciting. We longed to attend if possible. One morning we closed our school books to help load the rig with sleeping bags, camp kit and stove, food box, tent, stakes, pulpit, two benches, Bible box, medicine kit, Berno, Inocencia, five Knights and Perky, the pup.

Upon arriving at San Felix, they let us stay in the *old casa de hacienda*. A palm thatched roof on walls of bamboo, plastered with chopped straw mixed with mud, didn't keep all the little creatures out. We looked carefully for tarantulas and scorpions, especially in the evening when they made their nightly foray.

We held classes during the day. In the evening we had song services, taught flannelgraph lessons, and Roscoe preached in Aymara. People came to know the Lord and all were encouraged.

During the morning while I cooked soup for the day, the girls played with their dolls. Those dolls were the perfect advertisement for the meetings.

"Let me see," Aymara mamas whispered, wanting to hold them.

"It feels like skin," they exclaimed, as they rubbed the arms and legs. "They see and sleep!" They giggled as they rocked the dolls back and forth to watch the eyes open and close.

"Feel it, their hair is real." Losing their fear, they talked more loudly, completely fascinated with such babies.

Satisfied that the dolls weren't real babies, they reached to feel the girls' hair. Delighted with such silky, soft, blond curls—a complete contrast to their own coarse, black braids—they couldn't keep from touching them, much to Beverly's consternation.

"Bevie, don't pull back," I admonished. "They won't hurt you."

"But Mommie, their hands might not be clean." She had a point, for I also feared head lice, since they often picked lice from each others' heads.

As for Karen, she didn't think about unclean hands and thoroughly enjoyed the attention.

What about the tent meetings? The Lord blessed again and added new ones to the church in San Felix. In later years we learned that the presence of our children in meetings set a good example for the brethren.

Within the first year in the Yungas we realized the little one-pole army tent was not large enough, so wrote to the States for a larger one.

"Watch your finances," the mission board responded. "There's no money in the north now. Cut back on your expenses."

"Don't they realize how the work is growing?" I was bitterly disappointed.

"I'm sure they do, but if they have no funds and we are to have a bigger tent, the Lord will provide." The excitement and growth of the work strengthened Roscoe's faith.

The Lord did provide. He worked in the hearts of Christian Endeavor young people, who raised money for a 20 by 30-foot tent.

Now we launched into towns and bigger communities. In Coripata over 700 crowded into, and around, the new tent each night. Eighty-seven new converts made a start with the Lord but many dropped out. Nevertheless, those who remained formed the nucleus of a church.

A rowdy bunch listened in Huancané, but some accepted. The most rambunctious accused us of sleeping on our feet when we prayed.

Ilumaya sets on top a mountain ridge. "We'll start early," Roscoe told Berno. "They say it is a two and a half hour hike up the mountain. They will have mules waiting for us at the bridge below."

Next day, early afternoon found Roscoe and Berno following mules loaded with tent equipment up a zig-zag, rocky path—up,up,up. They pitched the tent on a knoll, with a beautiful view of the river far below and purple folds of Andean mountains stretching far to the horizon.

Along with a beautiful spot for meeting, the Lord touched hearts in Ilumaya. As Roscoe preached and Berno gave the story of the Prodigal Son, two prodigals responded. After asking Jesus to forgive them, Francisco and Clemente, brothers, knelt in the dust, facing each other, and with arms entwined they asked pardon—the first time they had spoken to each other in seven years.

Francisco told the story later. "Seven years ago, Clemente and I had words. I was angry. So was he. We vowed never to speak to each other again. Since Papá is gone, we must tend the family farm. When I needed to tell him something about the land, I spoke to Mamá. She told him. And likewise Mamá brought messages to me from Clemente. We avoided each other, although we lived in the same house—he upstairs and we down."

"Now we can talk. Thank you for coming." Clemente's tearful expression of thanks touched all, as he gave Roscoe a strong *abrazo* (embrace).

True brothers again after seven years

New converts

A Prayer of Faith

"Don't leave us. We need to learn how to walk," Ponciano pleaded after the first tent meeting.

On the last night of the meeting, new believers chose their leader and Roscoe promised to come back the following week to teach them.

"God's word is truth. Our entire message is based on this book," Roscoe emphasized, as he held up his Bible. "Buy a Bible. You must have one, for that is God's word to us."

"I have a Catholic Bible, pastor. Is that okay?" Ruperto asked.

"Yes, bring it. It has the same message as the evangelical Bible."

They learned how to use the Bible—how to find texts, how to read written texts (chapter three, verse sixteen, was written 3:16), the importance of memorizing the books of the Bible so they could find their texts, the difference between the Old and New Testaments, and of course, the truths of the Bible.

Along with learning the teachings of the Word, they learned how to apply those truths to their own lives.

"Pastor, what does the Bible say about praying to the virgin Mary and the saints?"

"The Bible says we are saints. It also says there is only one mediator between God and man—Jesus Christ."

This led to a discussion about church history, how the custom of worshipping saints began. All agreed that this was idolatry.

"What about celebrating All Saints' Day (Halloween)?" someone timidly asked. Several snickered.

"That's a good question," Roscoe responded. "What is the significance of this *fiesta*? Why do you celebrate?"

"The souls of the dead come back to earth and we must give them food for their travels," Antonio explained boldly.

"What happens if you don't give them food?"

"They cry if we don't take food to the cemetery. They will torment us by making us sick or causing our crops to fail or...." Many spoke at once.

Pablo explained in more detail. "My mother is dead. It would show disrespect if I didn't take a plate of steaming hot soup to put on her grave, light a candle, and pray for her."

"The rich have money so they can hire someone to pray for their dead," someone added.

"I always leave a stalk of sugar cane so my brother can use it as a walking cane in his travels," Luisa contributed to the explanation.

"*Bueno*," Roscoe interrupted the conversation. "Good. Now let's see what the Bible says about this. Open your Bibles to Luke 16:20—page 951."

He paused a bit, so all could find their text. After reading and explaining the story of the rich man and Lazarus, he concluded, "No, no one can come back from either Heaven or Hell. Scripture says, '...it is appointed unto men once to die, and after this the judgement.'" He waited a bit longer while slow readers finished the text.

"No, souls do not come back to earth on All Saints' Day. This *fiesta* is not for believers. It is no sin to take flowers to the cemetery in remembrance of your loved ones but leaving food, thinking souls will be back, and praying for them, does no good."

Some believed. Others showed signs of doubt but said nothing.

"I have a question," Ruperto raised his hand. "What happens when a baby dies if it doesn't have a name and hasn't been baptized? Our little boy died before he was baptized and he had no name." The silence could be felt, for all had experienced similar circumstances.

"There's nothing in scripture that says a baby goes to *limbo* if it dies without a name," Roscoe explained. Knowing Aymara culture, he explained further: "In fact, the word *limbo* isn't mentioned in the Bible. There is no such place as limbo. Babies with names or without names go to be with Jesus when they die."

"You mean they aren't angry with us and aren't up there making hail pellets to throw down on our fields?"

"No, that is false. When your baby dies, it is innocent. It is not guilty of sin, so it goes to Heaven."

Many sighed with relief.

"And purgatory?" someone whispered softly.

"The Bible doesn't speak of purgatory either. The word isn't in the Scriptures. We either go to Heaven or to Hell. We make the choice. There is no in-between place."

Questions like these described the fear that had bound these Aymaras for many centuries. Now, they were free. As they went out into the night, they began singing a new chorus—"*Cristo rompe las cadenas*—Christ breaks the chains of sin and sets me free."

Singing is a joyful addition to the Aymara Christian culture. The believers learned the old hymns of the church and the happy choruses by their numbers in the book, not by the titles. They spent at least an hour each meeting singing old favorites: "What a Friend," "Power in the Blood," "Beulah Land," "When the Roll is Called up Yonder," and many others.

Everyone who believed bought a Bible and hymnbook, whether or not they could read. It was a status symbol—a testimony to the world. Many learned to read from those two books.

"Where are you going tonight, Daddy?" the children frequently asked at the Monday breakfast table.

"Tonight I go to Pichu. Tomorrow night to Chaco again. Wednesday to the logging camp. Thursday to Ticuniri. And Friday we start another tent meeting, this time in Florida."

"Yesterday there were only 21 at Chaco for service. Where were the others?" I asked.

"An engineer came from La Paz to measure land last week and of course, as is the custom, they had a *fiesta* and several got drunk. Now they feel ashamed to come back to service."

"Someone needs to visit them, to encourage them." "Yes, I know. We really need a national pastor, several national pastors. This job is too big for one man."

"It sounds to me like discipling new Christians is harder work than getting them converted," I commented.

We scheduled our week with this thought in mind: four nights discipling, two nights in tent meetings and two services on Sunday—eight meetings a week.

One Monday it poured rain all day. The raging river below turned chocolate brown.

"I'm taking my sleeping bag, honey. If the road slides in, I'll just stay at Pichu. Don't worry." Roscoe gave us a hug and went up the ravine for meeting.

After reading a chapter from the life of famous missionary Mary Slessor and another from *Egermeir's Bible Stories for Children*, we all knelt along the divan for nightly prayers. Tonight each one voiced an oft repeated prayer, "bring Daddy home safely."

While the kids washed their teeth at the water faucet on the veranda, I carried a kerosene lantern upstairs to search the walls and floor for scorpions. Often, shortly after sundown, they came under the roofing tiles, then down the walls and on to the floor.

When the children were asleep and I had turned out the light, I listened to the roar of the river, boulders tumbling with the force of the water, while rain swept under the tiles to sprinkle my face.

I wonder where Roscoe is? Lord, please take care of him. I drifted off to sleep, hoping he wasn't trapped along the road between slides.

At 5:30 a.m. Perky barked. Soon Roscoe walked in.

"I had to leave the car up the road a couple of miles. I'll go back to get it when trucks start coming through."

"Such is life in the Yungas. I have no complaints. I'm just glad you are home safely. Did you have a good meeting?" I inquired.

"Uh-huh, very good, but we have a problem up there. No one in that group reads except Alejo's ten-year-old son, Eulogio. Alejo has offered to teach the Sunday School lesson. He says Eulogio will read the lesson to him, then he will teach. They need a lot of prayer."

Next morning I pulled the drapes aside to see clouds of fog hanging low up the gorge, completely obscuring the mountain we called Old Faithful. I knew the black slate still pierced the blue sky. I knew the immovable mountain still stood sentinal over our canyon. When clouds of discouragement crept down upon us, however, the sight of Old Faithful reminded us that God was still standing with us, even though hidden by clouds of problems.

"Lo, I am with you always," He promised, so we took heart and pressed on.

For us "pressing on" meant planting churches in new areas, discipling believers, encouraging the discouraged, helping to pick up the fallen, being a listening ear for those with problems, and just being there. It also meant refusing to worry and fret over something we could not change. It meant forgetting the past and accepting the challenge of what lay beyond the next ridge, on down the river, or around many curves to the end of the road.

Together we read *Behind the Ranges*, a story of church planting among the Lisu, a tribe in southwest China. Lisuland and the Yungas are similar, both in topography and people.

The story challenged Roscoe to launch out in faith for souls in the Yungas. "If God can work miracles for the Lisu, He can work miracles in Aymaraland."

He reported to the mission board:

A full Yungas program tends to tie us up in visitation, classes, and conferences, but we can never losesight of the call to evangelize and reach every corner of the Yungas with the Gospel. I have felt led to advance much in the prayer of faith these days and am asking and expecting from Him, 1000 souls during our first term here, 20 established church groups and 10 church buildings. Humanly speaking, this is absurd, but thank God, this work isn't of human origin and I am convinced that God delights in the seemingly impossible. Will you join with us in prevailing prayer that God will

send a mighty awakening among these people?
He also wrote to his father:

Dad, I want you to be my prayer partner in this step of faith for a special outpouring of the Holy Spirit. The Yungas work is one of faith, not for funds, but for God's convicting and keeping power. With almost no trained workers, we rest in the Lord. Do pray the Lord of the harvest to send forth laborers into His harvest.

New Christians at tent meeting

On Down the Trail

A Busy Day

The Lord blessed and within five months of our arrival in the Yungas, seven new church groups were meeting. We tried to encourage them by frequent visits but Arapata got few visits, for they were three hours away in dry weather, and that meant six hours driving time and four hours in services—two in the morning and two in the afternoon.

On a Sunday we left home by seven a.m. We always took a lunch, even though we might not need it—little potatoes boiled in their jackets, catsup to dip them in, Spam sandwiches, carrot sticks and cookies. The believers usually supplied our desserts of bananas, oranges, tangerines, papaya, avocado or whatever was in season.

After service people crowded around the Travelall to buy Bibles and hymnbooks or to ask for free tracts or medicine.

We carried the medicine kit every place we went. Often people called Roscoe "doctor".

"Doctor, my baby has a fever and diarrhea."

"Pastor, I cough and spit blood."

"Pastor Raúl, my son, Alejandro, doesn't eat well. What can I do for him?"

"*Hermano*, remember you gave my son medicine for parasites a couple of months ago. Well, he got rid of 600. I counted them," Tomás proudly informed us.

"My tooth aches, pastor, I can't sleep." A mama motioned to her jaw wrapped in a not-too-white rag knotted on top of her head.

So Roscoe treated them all, then pulled the tooth, without anesthesia. She groaned a bit; Roscoe waited a spell, still keeping a tight grip on the tooth with his dental forceps. Another gentle twist, another groan, he waited again, wiggled it a bit more, then out it came.

"Here it is." Roscoe dropped it in the outstretched corner of her shawl. She proudly showed it to all who watched, which included strangers who had stopped along the road to observe this fascinating dentist.

"I remember the first tooth I pulled," Roscoe reminisced as he dropped the forceps into the medical kit. "It wasn't too successful. I didn't know how to gently twist, then wait, and repeat the process. Instead, I just pulled up real hard. When the tooth came out, it took the skin off my own nose, much to my chagrin and the amusement of all those who were watching."

Sometimes people asked for help regarding life-threatening situations, or those beyond hope. Many times these requests came from people outside the church, like the man who was bitten by a snake while gathering wood down by the river. The blood and poison surged through his body while rapidly climbing the hill to his house. Of course we could do nothing for him.

But our help, whether successful or not, witnessed for the Lord. Many came to know Him because of that little fishing-tackle box that became a medicine kit.

Because of such delays along the road, we often arrived back home well after 10 p.m., tired but thankful to be of help to others. Because of the heavy load we realized that we had to have help. We couldn't do it alone.

"Lord, send us workers," we constantly pleaded. "You've told us to `pray the Lord of the harvest to send forth laborers into the harvest.'"

We waited. Things got worse. Loggers moved away. Some believers backslid. They had no one to teach them. Braulio became sick so went back to the altiplano. Cipriano quit teaching in Arapata and returned to La Paz to learn a trade. We had no help and we were discouraged. We experienced the stark truth that it is much easier to bring people to repentance than to establish them in their walk with the Lord.

We wrote to our family in the north:

"We are having problems pastoring these seven new churches," We don't know what to do. Should we stop having tent m e e t - ings and not evangelize any more new communities so we can spend more time teaching these new ones, until they are strong enough to stand alone? Or should we forge ahead evangelizing, leaving the new believers to the Holy Spirit and hope they don't fall. Those who teach indigenous church growth principles say, "Don't pastor. Leave the new ones to the nationals". But when we don't have national leaders, what do we do? Our faith is

being tried these days, but surely the Lord is
able to keep them.

"Maybe we'd better not have any more tent meetings," I suggested. "Winning people to the Lord, then
watching them flounder in their walk and drop away is
discouraging."

"Don't we believe God answers prayer?"

"I'm sure He does, but obviously He isn't answering
now."

"Oh yes, He is. He says 'wait'."

So we did. We waited several months while con-
tinuing in meetings night after night.

With the help of flannelgraph lessons they saw themselves.

"Some seed falls on the road, some falls on rocky soil,
some falls in the weeds, and some falls in good soil.
Which are you?"

Many were the rocky soil and persecution drove
them away because they were not rooted in the Word.
We had no workers to teach them.

During those months we read the stories of Mueller,
Taylor, Goforth and Fraser—men of great faith and missionary vision.

"Attempt enough to need God in your program,"
Taylor said. We did. We cast ourselves on the Lord, rec-
ognizing it was His work, not ours.

"It's the work of the Holy Spirit to teach and keep
these new believers," we reminded ourselves.

Ten months passed. We continued to evangelize,
disciple, encourage, and to remind God that we needed
help—national workers. God heard and answered.
When the Copajira Bible School was out in July, seven
enthusiastic students asked to help in the Yungas. They
wanted to be involved in teaching, discipling and

pastoring. However, after one year, most went back to the altiplano, giving various excuses for leaving.

"I don't like to walk up and down mountains trails."

"My wife won't come to the Yungas to be with me."

"Too much hard work, and it's discouraging when people drop out of the church."

"I need more money."

"There are too many bugs."

"I can't take the heat."

So we learned that workers come and workers go. When they go, the load is heavier for the missionary, but the Holy Spirit never leaves. He is the keeper, teacher and encourager.

Scriptures say the Sabbath should be a day of rest, but our Sabbaths were anything but restful. In fact, they were the most tiring day of the week. After one such weekend I wrote to friends in the north:

> We left at 7:30 a.m. After stopping at Sacahuaya to pick up a wheelbarrow, we drove on to the bridge where we picked up two believers. We stopped at Chajjro to leave a kitten for a believer and pick up four more believers, then stopped along the road to pick up Pastor Silva and his daughter, Carmen, who were walking the seven miles to Huancapampa for service. They make this trip every Sunday.
>
> At Huancapampa, we made plans to dedicate a baby on our way back at five p.m., then went on down to Parascato to leave Berno for services and finally back up to Chulumani, where we had two services, one in the morning and another at two o'clock in the afternoon.

As usual, we were late leaving Chulumani, went down after Berno, back up to Huancané to deliver the wheelbarrow and to see how they were progressing on their new church building. Several people wanted medicine so we gave a few shots and didn't leave until 7 p.m.—already two hours late.

We hurried on to Huancapampa to find the brethren still waiting for the baby dedication. These new believers think it very important to dedicate their babies. They have been taught that if babies haven't been baptized (dedicated), and then die, they will go to limbo. Many still believe there is a place where babies suffer after death.

We had service until nine p.m., then arranged for the wedding of the couple whose baby we dedicated. On the way h o m e w e dropped believers off at various places, arriving at ten. Too tired to eat supper, we just fell into bed. A long busy day!

People often didn't marry legally in the Yungas when we arrived. Because the Yungas is so isolated and because the notary's fee was expensive, people just started living together, with no thought of marrying. When people came to know the Lord, however, they felt the need to live within the law. A part of our discipling was to help with weddings.

"Alejo and Manuela want to be married on Tuesday," Roscoe announced after service one Sunday. "We'll take them to Yanacachi, the county seat, for the civil ceremony by the notary."

As usual, the notary arrived late so we waited three hours.

"Will the witnesses please stand and swear that these two are single," he mumbled in a toneless voice.

"But Sir," Juan, a new believer pleaded, "we are evangelicals and as such, we cannot swear. See, Christ Himself said so." He whipped out a little New Testament from his pocket to show the underlined words of Matthew 5:33-37.

"Let me see," the notary said gruffly, while reaching for the Testament to carry it to the open door for better light. Adjusting his glasses farther down his nose, he read the words half aloud.

"You're right," he nodded. "It does say, 'swear not at all'. So you can't be a witness if you can't take an oath. We'll just have to go out on the street to find another who can."

Alejo and Manuela looked bewildered. Juan looked disappointed. The notary turned palms up and looked helpless.

Roscoe promptly explained the Biblical view of oaths, but the notary still wasn't convinced. After shuffling papers while mumbling to himself, however, he proceeded with the ceremony, then held out his hand for the legal fee.

Back at our home in Waicani, Roscoe married them again with a Christian ceremony, then prayed for this newly married couple who had been living together for 20 years. Now they testified that they knew God approved of their union.

Alejo's house was a thatched bamboo shack below the road, just big enough to sleep five people. Manuela cooked in a tiny lean-to kitchen around the side of the hut. Even in their poverty, they gave generously of all they had, both time and possessions. Custom demanded a celebration after the wedding, but fortunately, they broke tradition and opted not to serve a big meal to all the community.

Alejo and Manuela's wedding sparked many more in our churches. Many people expressed an interest, but some wanted to wait to "see if it works for Alejo." This was unknown territory for everyone.

Some of those who did marry planned a big wedding. One was a double wedding, with all the children and grandchildren helping with the celebration. It was an all-day affair, with many neighbors invited.

After the usual civil ceremony with the notary, the newlyweds gathered with neighbors and family to sing, give testimonies and be married the second time.

Afterwards came the big feast: vegetable soup with fat toasted pasta floating in it, chicken in hot sauce over rice, fried bananas, boiled bananas, mashed *chuños* mixed with hot sauce, and orange juice.

Roscoe drank the first glass of juice, then the glass was passed to all 26 guests without being washed between times.

"That was good juice," he commented, as he went out to find Gary, who was hunting birds with his slingshot.

Coming around the corner of the house, Roscoe found a fellow   squeezing oranges with his hands. His method was unique---he peeled the orange first, then squeezed the pulp through his fingers. Now and then he coughed that dry hacking cough known so well in the Yungas.

I've given that fellow medicine for TB, Roscoe thought, then promptly forgot about calling a son to eat.

Not all weddings were peaceful celebrations.

Santiago was one of the Bible School students who stayed in the Yungas to help. He had the most difficult pastoral situation. He pastored five small groups within a five-mile area, up and down the mountain. He was a circuit-hiker during the week, then on Sunday all his parishioners gathered at Chacala for meeting.

In the midst of church activities, Santiago's eye caught an attractive young lady and before too long they were planning marriage.

Unfortunately, they planned their wedding for a week we were busy in tent meetings. But it helped to have Leland and Iverna Hibbs and boys visiting at that time.

Back at the bride's home on the mountain side, after a civil ceremony, Santiago and Elena entertained royally with the usual meal and drinks. People wandered in and out, congratulating them, while pinning money to a money-tree and placing flower petals on their heads.

"Berno and I need to leave so we can get back to the meeting tonight," Roscoe whispered to Leland in early afternoon. "Take us to the end of the road, then you can come back for the girls."

No wedding is complete without much singing. As I played the accordion, the guests sang on and on, while our men folk disappeared down the mountain.

"Get out of my way!" someone yelled as he shoved three or four fellows aside, trying to enter the room.

"My brother is drunk," Elena whispered in my ear, then glanced about with a desperate fear in her eyes.

"I don't want that *gringa* in my house. Get her out," he ordered in a drunken garbled speech. When some tried to hold him, a scuffle resulted.

The brethren feared for our safety, so Iverna and I slipped out to await Leland on the road below. We didn't want to leave Santiago and Elena but our departure lessened tension and left the guests to wish them many happy years in the Lord's work.

Sometimes our appointments almost overlapped as they did the day we helped Sacahuaya believers dedicate their new church building. We hurried home; Roscoe gobbled his dinner, then left to keep another appointment—that of taking another bride and groom and witnesses to be married by the notary.

"I should be back by four o'clock." He waved and was gone. Hours later we saw the lights of the Travelall, as it swung around the curves down the canyon.

"After the wedding at the church, a new believer came with two little kids to be dedicated," he explained, as he ate a bowl of soup and one of Inocencia's freshly baked rolls. "I don't like to dedicate children just because parents are afraid they will get sick and die, so we had another service to explain what dedication is all about. They need to know that dedication isn't necessary as far as heaven is concerned. Dedication is really for parents."

"It's been a long day," I commented, picking up the soup bowl to stack it in the sink. "First, we started with a church dedication, then a wedding, afterwards, a child dedication, and finally, a service to disciple new believers."

The words echoed in the empty room, as we carried the light upstairs to bed. We were tired and needed a vacation.

Knight family on trail

On Down the Trail

Ants or Molasses

A rule of the mission requires all missionaries to take a month's vacation every year. But sometimes it took more nervous energy to go on vacation than to stay at home and work.

We took such a trip in 1957, right after Christmas. This time we opted for a vacation in Arica, Chile. "We'll go by the farm, down through Arequipa, Peru and on down south to Arica," Roscoe explained as we poured over maps.

"Can we go swimming, Daddy? Can we take the life boat? How long will we have to ride? When do we leave?" Questions came thick and fast as we made plans.

"We'll leave right after Christmas, but first we must get permits to leave the country."

It was no trifling matter to get a permit. "I'm sorry, *Señor* Knight, but the first thing you need to do is to put up a $3000.00 bond in order to take your car out of the country. Or maybe you can get someone to guarantee you won't sell it outside Bolivia." Officials were always very matter of fact people who seemed to think that money was easy to come by.

In Latin America certain legal advisors are essential. So we went to see our lawyer, *Señor* Miranda, asking him to explain the situation.

"Yes, I understand you don't have $3000.00 in the bank, but write the check. You will get it back when you return. Don't mention to the captain of the customs house that you don't have the money," Miranda warned. "He just wants to be sure the vehicle will come back. I trust you, so I will guarantee your check."

Then Roscoe wrote the only bad check of his life. He also obtained the permit to drive the car across the border.

"We'll drive to the farm to spend the night with the Willcutses," I explained to three jubilant kids who were feeling confined in La Paz with nothing to do. Even our bumping in and out of chuck holes and arriving in a hail storm didn't dampen their enthusiasm.

The next morning we started on our way. Between Copajira and Desaguadero on the Peruvian border are twenty miles of what we thought was the worst road in Bolivia, until we moved to the Yungas. This bone-crusher ran along the shore of Lake Titicaca for part of the way so the beautiful, quiet, pastoral view of lake activity diverted our attention from all the jolts.

"Look, Daddy, look at the *balsas* (reed boats)," Gary shouted from the back seat of the Travelall. "Remember when I rode in one with Casimero at Amacari and we got a lot of *chokas*?"

"Uh-huh," Roscoe nodded as he tried to ride the ridge between deep ruts made by the trucks."

Cattle, standing up to their bellies in the brackish water along the shore, fed on *totora*, a tall lake reed. *Chocas*, yellow-billed mudhens, swam among the cattle, often diving for some choice tidbit. A sodden *balsa* or two were discarded on shore and newer ones under sail plied the water while their owners let down nets for fish.

"That's the world of today," I waved my hand toward the lake. "Some are oblivious of problems around them; just carrying on as their ancestors have for centuries."

"Then there are others like us," Roscoe interrupted, "with more modern conveniences, battling the elements to run a race with a clock. The customs house closes at noon."

We pulled up before a small hole-in-the-wall room. Roscoe ducked his head to enter, then stood before a desk, hat in hand, adjusting his eyes to the darkness. Here he failed to reckon with government inefficiency.

"*Señor* Knight," the soldier at the desk spoke bruskly, "you say there has been a change in the law and you don't need a visa to enter Peru, but we haven't heard of such a change." He slapped his book shut and with the disdain of a newly appointed secretary, dismissed the case.

"Please sir, I understand your position," Roscoe spoke kindly with not a hint of frustration, as was his usual method of dealing with government officials. "I'm not asking you to do something you shouldn't, but this is what they told me in La Paz. May I speak to the Captain?"

The Captain offered to send a telegram to find the truth of this new law, so we waited six hours for an answer. *Then* they told us the telephone line was down to Puno, Peru, and we'd have to go back to La Paz for our visas.

Since a bright side usually looms with every problem we began to search for it. As we started back to Copajira, we drove through Guaqui, a port town on the lake shore.

"Hey, I believe there's a Peruvian Consul here," Roscoe exclaimed. He was right.

Next morning after spending another night with Willcutses, we started again for Arica, armed with the proper visas and car permit.

We arrived in Puno late afternoon, having driven all day around the shores of Lake Titicaca. It was a beautiful view but a miserable road. Here again our plans were dashed. Peru required another $3,000.00 bond for the car. We knew no one in Puno to guarantee for us, so we expected to go back to La Paz, thinking our vacation was over.

Suddenly the customs agent phoned someone, telling him the situation—we were missionaries on vacation, needing a guarantee. This kind, unknown person came to our rescue. He wrote our guarantee because we were missionaries and because Roscoe knew an Adventist missionary, a friend of our unknown friend. Their paths had crossed as they waited at a mudslide in the Yungas some months before. Coincidence? No. At that moment we were sure that God even works through unknown friends and mudslides.

We praised the Lord as we drove out of town to find a spot, fix a bite to eat, and then bed down for the night. Fixing the bite to eat was simple. The process of crawling into our sleeping bags was a bit more difficult. We pushed the gasoline barrel and back seat under the car, then deposited three suitcases, food and tool boxes, life raft, and water jug up front and around the edges. This made sleeping room for four in the back, while

Karen slept on the front seat. It was a snug fit, but fun when on vacation.

The next morning as the sun peeked over Lake Titicaca, we broke the ice to wash our faces. We climbed to over 15,000 feet, then jolted across the top of the cold, barren Andean range all day—up and down, up and down—over an extremely bumpy, corrugated road.

In spite of the rough road there was much to see: hundreds of pink flamingos standing on tall, spindly, black legs in crystal clear lakes, flamingo nests built of mud in the shallow water and a large salt lake where people mounded piles of salt to be sacked for market. At last we topped a 14,000-foot crest to look down across a desert wasteland and into the valley of Arequipa.

Here we hit the pavement—the only paved road in our 600-mile trip. Our troubles ended—or so we thought.

We arrived at the Chilean-Peruvian border, only 20 miles from our destination, in early afternoon, thinking we had plenty of time to get across the border before nightfall.

"What's the problem?" I asked as Roscoe came back from the customs office looking a bit discouraged.

"The customs agent, who has to stamp our papers, is gone to celebrate the day. It's the Day of the Kings, you know, the day they believe the wisemen brought gifts to baby Jesus."

"Oh, no..." we all groaned.

"There's nothing else to do but find a place to park and spend another night by the side of the road."

The problems of vacation travel soon vanished from memory in the cold Antarctic current in Arica bay. Gary learned to swim by diving off Roscoe's shoulders, then swimming to shore. The girls were more fearful of the water. Today all three cherish Dinky Jeeps, a souvenir of a happy vacation on the Chilean coast. In spite of all the problems, that vacation gave us the lift we needed.

Another year we decided to spend our vacation down Caranavi way, about 2,000 feet altitude but malaria infested. This little village of approximately 300 people, lost under a canopy of jungle trees occupied a sandy beach at the end of a new road. Our real reason for going was to investigate the possibilities of a future tent meeting in that area; however, we took advantage of the trip and spent a few days relaxing.

"My, it's hot," I complained, as I fanned and swatted fruit flies that left red welts on my legs. The girls wore jeans to protect their legs but that wasn't acceptable dress for me.

We pitched our tent by the river, hoping for a breath of cool air. It would also make it easier for swimming.

"Come in, Mommie. The water's warm." The girls tugged at my arms, but I looked down along the river and couldn't see one woman wearing a swimming suit. I hesitated.

Swimsuits were indecent for Aymara women but they were considered modest in only a thin slip. No one gave them a second glance. I didn't like the idea of being seen in a sopping slip clinging to my skin.

In the heat of high noon, while sitting on an air mattress writing letters in the shade of the tent, I glanced up to see everyone having fun in the water. There was Rosa, our maid, in black *bombochas*—black bloomers like grandmother wore. She wasn't the least bit embarrassed. That did it. I changed to a skirt and blouse to join the crowd. No one glanced my way, except the kids who thought I didn't look quite right for the water.

I glanced across the river and saw some fellow bathing, with not a stitch on. Local people customarily went to the river, took off their clothes and washed them. While the clothes were spread over the rocks to dry, they bathed. Then they dressed in their damp clothes and went on their way.

That's a simple way to do it, I thought, *take a bath and do the laundry all at the same time. Why do we make things so complicated?* I dropped down into the water to savor the fun with the family.

Another time when we went to Caranavi on vacation, we pitched our tent in the jungle, about five miles from the river. Swimming wasn't so handy, but there were fewer people.

Having just finished nine consecutive weeks of meetings, we were tired. Roscoe had spent one of those weeks in La Paz, meeting with the executive council of the national church; then he went on to the farm to help solve farm problems, a much more tiring work than evangelistic meetings in the Yungas.

Anyway, we needed a rest and thought Caranavi would be a wonderful place to do nothing. But, alas! We ended up having five services and one wedding during that time. We simply could not escape meetings when the brethren knew we were close by.

We pitched our tent under giant hardwood trees. Since the tent was large enough to serve as an entire house, we set up a pup tent in one end where Gary and Beverly slept. We parked the Travelall in the middle of the tent. This was the master bedroom, with Karen sleeping on the front seat. The kitchen and an army cot where Rosa slept occupied the other end of the tent.

Everything was organized except time. We didn't live by the clock. We ate when we were hungry, slept when sleepy, and just did as we pleased. Well, mostly......

"Mommie, I'm going hunting."

"Okay, Gary, but don't be gone long or we'll wonder about you." Of course, he was gone too long. But those hunts proved profitable. He shot parrots, toucans and a squirrel with his pellet gun, sometimes killing them.

"Can we eat the parrot, Mommie?"

"If you or your daddy will clean it, I'll cook it in the pressure cooker. But I warn you, it will be tough." It was.

Sometimes he brought his game back alive. This presented other problems, especially for Gary if he tried to hold on to an injured squirrel.

"How did it happen?" Daddy inquired, as he examined bites on Gary's arm and leg.

"I didn't think it would bite. When I just stunned it with the bullet I thought I'd pick it up and keep it for a pet, but then it began to fight and bite, and I just about didn't hang on to it."

"Well, son, I think we need to take you down to Caranavi to the clinic and ask a doctor's advice. I'm sure there is rabies out here in this jungle."

"I don't think there's any danger," the doctor advised after the five mile drive to town. "Besides, we don't have any rabies vaccine."

"Look what I brought home today." I heard Gary coming through the trees late one afternoon to show his trophy to the girls—a big toucan. Its huge curved bill was beautiful—shaded yellows blended into the black base.

"Save the bill for a souvenir," I encouraged. Carefully, he cut it away from the head, then laid it on the sloping roof of the tent to dry in the sun. "Your friends in the States will enjoy seeing it," I suggested, knowing full well that he was not enthusiastic about going to the States. The very mention of deputation left knots in his stomach. My suggestion ended in failure, for some unknown culprit stole the toucan bill during the night. Another day he had better success when he crippled a smaller toucan so took it home to add to our animal menagerie.

Along with the excitement of squirrels, parrots, and toucans, smaller inhabitants of the jungle visited us. *Polverines,* minute black fire gnats came in swarms each evening. They stung like fire! Of course, the ever-present fruit fly and the spotted deer fly made life miserable also.

It was still dark early one morning when we heard Cinders, our cocker spaniel, whining. He usually slept beside Rosa's cot but now he frantically raced in circles, stopping often to roll in the dirt, biting and scratching himself, then jumping high into the air.

He jumped on Rosa's bed. "Get off. Get out of here," she ordered, shoving him off.

Gary and Beverly awakened with a start when he bolted into their pup tent.

"Get out of here, you dumb dog!" Gary gave him a shove but Cinders had no intentions of being pushed out. Beverly felt something crawling so began sweeping the "something" off the sleeping bags.

"What's going on out there?" Roscoe grabbed a flashlight, opened the back door of the Travelall and was about to step down on the ground, when he noticed it was covered with a black flow of ants, looking very much like someone had dumped a barrel of molasses on the ground.

The ants were gone in about a half hour, but oh, the excitement they caused in passing through. Meanwhile, we sat in the Travelall reliving a frightening nightmare for Cinders.

The activity was hilarious—Cinders whining, Rosa beating her bed, Gary trying to kick the dog out of the pup tent, Beverly sweeping those crawling things away and all three hollering, "Ouch!".

When morning arrived a logger's wife, living in a hut nearby, informed us that our visitors were soldier ants who marched through the jungle as scavengers, to clean the jungle floor of insects or any dead carcasses of birds or snakes. And sometimes they attacked live chickens or dogs.

"It's better to sprinkle some ashes around your tent, for they will be back this afternoon," she advised.

She was right. They came, only to be met with fire.

"Careful, honey, we don't want to burn down the tent," I warned as Roscoe got out the gas can.

"I won't. But since we don't have ashes, I'll just pour a little gasoline along here and when they come, I'll drop a match in it. We'll see what happens," the man of the house declared, confident that his methods would work.

Later that evening we watched as wave after wave of ants were burned but still they kept coming. Finally, some found their way around the end of the wall of fire. They were determined not to let civilized man upset their God-given instincts. They swept through the tent and on across the jungle to their nest. They didn't realize they had added a bit of spice to a wonderful vacation, and provided an exciting topic for the next composition when school started.

Gary with toucan he shot

On Down the Trail

MK Education

Home schooling occupied an important place in our lives long before it was popular in the States. Every year we ordered a box of books and materials through the mail from Calvert Correspondence School.

Studying with Calvert provided the flexible schedule we needed to keep involved in missions. It meant we could close the books and go with Daddy to tent meetings. It meant we could go fishing at whatever time it fit his schedule. It also meant we could study as fast as we desired, a big advantage when we took a months' vacation in the middle of the school year.

Home schooling required strict discipline. School started at 8:30 in the morning; we usually finished by noon. A break for one of Rosa's cinnamon rolls and a drink provided time to stretch a bit but otherwise, there was no recess until we finished the lessons for the day.

Most of the time our one-room school functioned smoothly with three grades. We set our schedule to keep pace with schools in the States. On furlough the children entered the proper grades in public school, usually ahead of their peers.

Some people expressed a concern that missionary kids (MKs) didn't get a good education on the field. But hard work and discipline on our kids'part prepared them well. All three graduated from college with honors.

When Gary started the fifth grade, he had to be pushed to do his work.

"Gary, finish your work early. Remember, you have to do two lessons today. Thursday we will begin tent meetings. Those days you can play."

But Gary dawdled. The teacher reminded him often.

"It's clear that Gary isn't challenged with his studies this year, Roscoe," I said. "What can I do? I'm always hollering at him to `get busy'. I don't like that."

We discussed the situation, then by shortwave radio we talked with Leland and Iverna Hibbs at the mission farm.

"Yes, send him out. We'll be glad to have another son. Terry and Carol say there is plenty of room for another bed in their room."

We knew they didn't have room for another boy but the Hibbses proved to be good parents to a foster son. Gary was thrilled to go to the farm where the other missionary kids studied together.

"Bye-bye. We'll see you next month when we come out for council meeting." After a quick hug he ran off to play with the boys, and we were on our way back to the Yungas.

Those were busy days for Gary. He learned to drive the tractor. He climbed the mountain behind the farm to hunt chinchilla, then came home physically exhausted. He also hunted closer to home with his sling-shot and BB gun.

The boys built a tree house in a big eucalyptus tree, then carried their sleeping bags up the tree to spend the night. They shot doves, plucked and cooked them, then ate supper of partially cooked meat high in the tree house.

Easter presented a problem at the farm. Many Aymaras steal potatoes and barley on Saturday after Good Friday, for they think Jesus is dead so He can't see them. Since the farm always needed guards during this time, the missionary boys offered their services one year. They slept in a low straw hut, built in the middle of the potato field, to keep thieves at bay.

Aside from the results of a slingshot connecting with a fellow student and climbing a forbidden cliff, life was fun for Gary. The daily requirements of study and play, with enough work thrown in to make them responsible kids kept everyone happy.

Letters let us peek into a little boy's feelings.

Dear Daddy and Mommie,

I have been over to Orpha's (teacher) house this morning. I hit Marita with a clod, so we have been in a scrap ever since. I am having fun but I miss my pelet gun.

I'm not used to this kind of paper so you'll know why I can't make straight lines.

I get along alright but some times I wish you were here.

If you notis my righting is slopy its because I am in a hurry.

Lots of hugs and kisses
Gary

After a short time those monthly visits began to produce tears every time we left. A few at first, but the month before school was out, he sobbed and begged to go home with us.

"No, Gary, I think you'd better finish school out here. It's better that we finish what we start." Roscoe blinked away the tears as he hugged him. "We'll be back in another month then you can go home with us."

The girls and I wiped away tears as we drove off, leaving a homesick little boy.

When school let out and Gary had come back home to the Yungas, one morning he helped me do the washing, catching the clothes as they fell from the wringer into the rinse water.

"What happened at the farm? Why didn't you like school? Weren't Leland and Iverna good to you?"

"Oh, yeah, they were good to me." There was a long pause as he studied the water.

"Then what was the problem?" I urged.

"I didn't have any mommie or any daddy," he blubbered, as he burst into a flood of tears.

I gathered him into my arms and vowed that day never to send another child away from home at that early age.

Years later some have asked, "How did you teach your own children? What about discipline? I can't do it."

"It wasn't easy, but it was rewarding and even fun much of the time."

Roscoe gives a more realistic answer. "She was teacher during school hours and Mommie other times."

Home schooling for us meant the students could not sing in a chorus or participate in sports, since any ball other than a tether ball was lost down the mountain. There were other exciting activities to compensate for this. It isn't just any boy who can run out to kill a deer during recess.

"*Señor...Señor*, there's a deer up on the road," a neighbor boy yelled as he raced down to the house.

Roscoe grabbed his 30-30mm. He and Gary sped up the road while we girls watched the action from the yard.

"There it is, Daddy. See it?" Gary's sharp eye spotted it half hidden in the brush far below.

"When they shot it, it rolled clear to the river," I wrote to the folks in the States.

After reading my letter Gary corrected me. "No, you should say, `The gun blazed away and with a yell of excitement, we watched it roll down to the river.'"

At times like that I felt rewarded for the hours we spent writing compositions, which was not their favorite subject.   Of course book learning came to a halt that day, as Daddy taught a lesson on how to dress a deer---also a lesson about fairness and sharing.

"This portion is for the fellow who saw it first. This is for Juan, who came to tell us. Berno gets a big hunk for carrying it up that steep slope, almost straight up," Roscoe explained, as he gave each his share. Our portion was enough for our guests the next day when Robertses arrived.

That was a morning well spent. Next day we would go back to reading, writing, and arithmetic.

But again our day was interrupted. Some lessons are learned by hard experiences.

Lady's frantic barking announced a caller.

"Quiet, Lady," Roscoe commanded the dog, as he greeted neighbors from Pichu.

"*Señor*, we've come to borrow a lasso. A little boy is across the river and we need to pull him across."

Running to the storeroom to get the rope, Roscoe called over his shoulder, "Come on, Gary, let's go see if we can help."

On the way Alejo explained the situation.

"Salustio's little 9-year-old boy and his dog went down to the river to play. Apparently he took off his clothes to wash them. Evidently his dog fell in and he tried to rescue him, but fell in also. The river carried him about a kilometer downstream."

"Where are his folks?"

"Both went to La Paz with a load of produce—left him and his little sister alone."

"There he is over on that sandbar. See him?" Alejo pointed with his chin.

Roscoe stopped and the men cautiously picked their way down a perpendicular bank.

"Wait here, Gary."

One of the men fought the turbulent current to tie the rope around the little fellow, and all pulled the body across the   river. The men struggled to carry him up the bank to the car. Late that evening Roscoe told me about the tragic accident.

"After climbing the bank, I drew the cloth back to let Gary see, even though he looked bad. He was badly bruised. Every bone in his body was broken, and he had a big gash on the head. That will probably be the only warning that Gary will ever need about the danger of that treacherous river."

"I hope you're right. As for our school lessons today, experience often teaches more than books. But I hope we never have another lesson like that in our canyon."

Life went on. There were more pleasant lessons to learn. As part of their education the children had to take piano lessons long enough to play simple tunes and read music. Everyone was enthused about learning to play but the newness soon wore off. This laid the foundation for learning to play the accordion, trumpet and piano in later years.

There did come a time again when we had to send Gary and Beverly away to school. When Bevie was ready for high school, the two of them went to Tambo, the New Tribes school for missionary children, located in the Bolivian lowlands.

"How did they handle it?"

They got homesick, and we got lonesome. But sports helped Gary as he participated in cross-country racing and soccer.

"And Beverly?"

Let her tell it: "Every night after we went to bed, I heard someone crying, so softly I could barely hear it. We older girls weren't allowed to go into the little girls' room but that crying every night bothered me. One night after the dorm mother had gone, I tip-toed quietly into the room. I followed the sobs until I found her bed—just a tiny kindergartner, a long way from home, with no mommie to tuck her into bed at night. I hugged her, giving what comfort I could, then sneaked out."

Beverly could sympathize with that little one, for she too, was a bit homesick at times.

Oh, the price of MK education! It can be costly. Thankfully, Christmas provided the break when we could forget school and enjoy the season.

Christmas

Aymara believers in Bolivia looked forward to Christmas, that special time, with child-like anticipation. Their anticipation did not involve exchanging gifts or preparing big meals, for they did neither.

The church overflowed on Christmas eve when saints and sinners alike gathered to celebrate and to listen to the Christmas story in poetry, song, and drama. Young shepherds, wearing robes and bright turbans from a missionary closet, cradled newborn lambs. María only needed to take off her derby hat to play the part of Mary. She sat on the earthen floor by a mound of barley straw, gently jiggling a baby, wrapped in a colorful striped *ahuayo*. The daily life of the Aymara is a close parallel to that of the Jews in Jesus' day, making it easy to portray the Christmas story.

Not all actors are as innovative as one bright young Aymara playing the part of Herod in a palm-thatched bamboo church. Let's peek in on the scene:

Herod, with paper crown falling too low over one eye, is squatting on his haunches, when a servant announces a visitor.

A nervous wiseman enters, fidgeting with the tassel on his robe. Without a word of greeting, Mr. Wiseman lifts his eyes to the bamboo rafters and booms, "Where is He that is born King of the Jews?"

Poor Herod. He stands, prepared to return a greeting, but he can't remember his lines.

Silence.....

"Where is he that is born King of the Jews?" Again Mr. Wiseman repeats his question, this time with more emphasis.

Alas, Herod's mind is a blank.

Every resourceful Latin, however, has a favorite line in an emergency. Herod has no intention of going down in defeat. Lifting his head and looking Mr. Wiseman squarely in the eye, he commands, "Come back tomorrow!"

The wiseman is ushered out, while the crowd roars with   laughter.

The program made Christmas special for the Aymara christian. As for us missionaries, our hearts turned toward home. We missed the fun times with family and were a wee bit homesick.

The only memory I had of Christmas, other than school activities, was the Christmas morning when Mama died. Late that morning Daddy came home from the hospital with a decorated Christmas tree in one arm and dolls and a truck in the other. We sat on the floor around the tree to have Christmas.

As a child of nine years, I had no idea of the pain and broken heart that he was enduring. The indelible memory of that Christmas forced me to strive for meaningful traditions when Roscoe and I were married—ones that provided happy memories to pass on to our children.

But I didn't reckon with our lifestyle when we became missionaries. Living south of the equator meant Christmas in the summer time. Nasturtiums bloomed on our back wall, while the red, yellow, and green of the *kantuta*, the national flower, proudly displayed its colors of the Bolivian national flag. In the warm sun bees buzzed among the white alyssum and purple flowers of the myrtle hanging down the rock terrace. There was no snow, no Christmas trees, no decorated store windows. It didn't look like Christmas or feel like Christmas.

We experienced what we already knew, however. Christmas is of the heart. As we taught Aymara believers, it was a celebration of the birth of our Lord Jesus. This knowledge, plus simple traditions provide fond memories for today.

On a warm, balmy, summer evening at Christmas time fireflies flitted along the garden path. Through the open doors we heard the chatter of parrots, *uchis*, and *quehuays* as they settled for the night in the orange trees below the house. Bats darted from their dark sleeping quarters to catch night insects in flight. Far below, the river tumbled over boulders, providing a backdrop of sound for all the activity of the evening.

Inside, striving to keep alive the real meaning of Christmas, we gathered around the Christmas tree to read. With no radio, reading became our favorite pastime in the evenings. As we sipped egg nog, we sang carols, read the Christmas story and several favorites from the *Ideals* magazine—"'Twas the Night Before Christmas", "Willie and Annie's Prayer", "Jimmy's Letter to Santa Claus", Dicken's "A Christmas Carol", and others.

After smaller family members changed it several times, the tiny yellow singing bird finally perched on that perfect branch of the tree. The white angel, leaning as though he were listening to our reading, sparkled over the glossy leaves of the coffee tree, adorned with red berries and other tree ornaments. Reading certain Christmas stories became a tradition, but by necessity our tree was different almost every year. Before climbing the stairs to bed that night, we reminisced of past Christmases.

"I like our tree," I commented. "It looks like Oregon holly."

"Last year's tree was made with copper wire, shaped as graceful Japanese art. Daddy made it," one of the children remembered.

"Yeah, Mommie covered it with aluminum foil."

"I remember that it had clusters of tiny colored balls too." Karen always favored tiny things.

"One year when Hibbses were here for Christmas we cut a branch off Muñoz's evergreen." Gary remembered. "One branch was our whole tree."

"The evergreen growing behind the playhouse was our first Christmas tree in the Yungas," Daddy contributed to the discussion. "I bought it in La Paz; we planted it after Christmas."

"Would you like to hear about our first Christmas tree in Bolivia?"

"Yeah. Tell us about it, Mommie."

"Well, we spent our first Christmas in La Paz with the Chapmans. With everything new to us, we were interested in learning all we could about life in Bolivia. So when Ralph invited us to watch him make a Christmas tree, we followed him to the basement.

"'First, you find an old broomstick,' he explained, 'then you bore holes in it at just the right angles.'

"We watched as he prepared the broomstick, then helped stick evergreen branches into the holes. Presto! We had a perfect tree."

Christmas gifts came from the trunks and crates we took to Bolivia—dolls, a doll-house, Tinkertoys, a tow truck, a pellet gun, an HO train and much more.

Two unusual gifts however, came from my grandmother Arnett. She loved her children, grandchildren and great-grandchildren to the point of spoiling them.

"Spend the money on whatever you want," she instructed, as she handed us a check before we left the States.

So for our first Christmas in the Yungas, we bought a small upright piano.

The next Christmas she sent only $10.00, with the usual note, "Get something you need."

We thought and thought. We didn't need a thing.

"I know," someone suggested. (I can't remember who.) "Let's buy some cold cereal."

All agreed it was a good suggestion. We paid exorbitant prices: 60 cents for a box of Kix, 85 cents for Wheat Chex, 69 for Grape Nuts. Soon our $10.00 was gone, but we thought that gift the best we'd ever had.

After writing a thank-you note to Grandma, telling what we'd bought with her money, we received a reply with another $10.00 bill and a terse command, "Buy those kiddies all the cold cereal they want."

Grandma could never stand to see people hungry. With us so far from home, she was fearful we might not have enough to eat.

We spent the second $10.00 on a case of Wheaties, a Christmas gift that stretched throughout the year, even though it did become a bit stale and lifeless from the Yungas humidity.

149

One of the prized gifts from the crate was a big red wagon with Radio Flyer written on the side. That wagon lived up to its name and provided hours of fun.

The kids would pull the wagon to the top of our steep, narrow, rocky, and zigzag private road. Then all three would squeeze in and with Gary guiding, they would shove off. Many a time Roscoe and I heard that wagon bouncing over rocks, sliding around corners, gaining speed with every minute.

"Lean, Karen, lean," Gary urged, in order to have better success maneuvering the corners. But Karen, holding on to the sides of the wagon for dear life, insisted on sitting ramrod straight, while terror etched every muscle of her jaw.

Sometimes they didn't make the corner. But for the most part, we'd look up the road toward the water tank to see the wagon load of kids slide around that last curve, then screech to a halt only inches from the garage. We were convinced guardian angels were on duty.

Some gifts out of those crates weren't quite so daring. One year the girls got a doll house.

"Oh, look, tiny furniture!" Beverly squealed.

"And teeny babies!" Karen added, jumping up and down with delight. They were intrigued with their new gift but they felt a wee bit of jealousy, which forced them to learn the lesson of sharing.

"Whose house is it, Mommie?"

"It belongs to both of you."

"But, Mommie, she doesn't know how to play with it," Beverly complained. "She puts the bed in the kitchen."

True, Karen didn't know anything about arranging furniture; neither did she take good care of it. But she had lots of patience. She waited until Beverly wasn't playing with it, then rearranged the furniture to suit herself.

When Gary wanted to be included in the girls' play, he teased. If they weren't looking, he hid the babies in the chimney. Of course they were furious.

When they found the babies, he roared up with his fire-engine, yelling, "Your house is on fire. I'll put it out."

"No it isn't. Get out!" they ordered, without showing any sisterly love.

But he proceeded to put out the fire, then insisted their telephone needed fixing, much to the girls' consternation.

"Two's company and three's a crowd," was an old saying which proved true in our house. Such teasing caused friction but the three learned to play together peacefully, with a little help from parents.

Beverly was fussy about dirt, even as a small girl. When visiting away from home she had problems with the lack of sanitation and was never bold about eating just anything set before her. We called her our little nurse, so one Christmas she got a nurses' kit from Grandma.

"Karen, bring your babies to the clinic," Beverly commanded. "Let's see what's wrong with them."

Little babies and big babies lined up to go through the clinic.

"You have TB. You need a shot."

"Hold still. You have a bad case of *carachi* (impetigo) so I must cut some of your hair."

The nurse "shot", bandaged, and rubbed them with ointment until Mama Karen tired of that game. Then the nurse suggested one more common ailment.

"You need an x-ray, Mama. You're tired all the time so I'm sure you've got worms."

"Click, click, click." A few minutes later Karen received a hand-drawn x-ray, showing many different kinds of parasites. She paid her bill and walked out, clutching a bottle of foul-smelling worm pills.

It's easy to reminisce of the immediate family at Christmas time, but there were other activities that made the season special.

Every year we received an avalanche of Christmas cards. Some arrived as late as February by boat mail. At least half of them included letters; most everyone said they were praying for us.

"If prayer has any value at all," Roscoe commented, "this Yungas work can't fail."

It encouraged us to know that so many stood with us in planting Yungas churches.

The missionary family grew from five persons to six couples and seventeen children on the field at one time. We changed the place of our Christmas celebration as the need arose, from the La Paz mission house to the Copajira farm or to the Yungas. This depended upon the whim of new mothers when babies joined the group, or upon those who wanted to shop in La Paz. It also depended upon the courage of those who dared to brave Yungas roads in rainy season.

But certain things at Christmas time did not change. The inevitable cookies, homemade candy, and fruitcake signaled that the day was near.

There was nothing traditional however, about the kind of meat we served for Christmas dinner. Early in our missionary career we experienced our first disappointment with the meat. We could buy turkeys "on the hoof" at the meat market. They didn't drive them through the streets, selling from door to door as they did in Mexico City.

A farm girl all my life, I felt confident that we could pluck and clean a turkey. We should have questioned our wisdom when our co-workers refused to get involved, leaving us to spend three hours plucking pin feathers.

Of course, it was tough—the meat I mean. It taught me a lesson—all altiplano fowl must be cooked under pressure to be tender. But who likes boiled turkey for Christmas?

Thus, we changed the meat menu often. One year chicken roasted in the oven ten hours to become tender—and a bit dry. Other years, rabbit, Peking duck or fried chicken celebrated with us. Another time we bought three delicious hams with a $10.00 gift from a Women's Missionary Union. Perhaps the easiest Christmas dinner came through a generous gift from a Women's Missionary Union that paid the bill for the entire missionary family to enjoy dinner at the Sucre Palace Hotel. What luxury!

Due to the advance of poultry technology in the Yungas, we took seven capons out for Christmas dinner one year. But the day we were to help eat the birds, we got stuck in a mudslide and almost missed the dinner.

Travel presented a problem during that season of the year. Once Jack and Gerry Willcuts were two hours late to dinner at the farm. Roscoe and Paul Cammack found them stuck about ten miles away. Gerry had gotten out of the Jeep, her feet slipped, and she sat down in the mud in her new Christmas dress. Of course she cried. But we had a happy celebration afterwards.

Oscar and Ruth Brown and Gene and Betty Comfort and boys   braved the Yungas roads one Christmas, only to be stopped by a slide. They left their Jeep above Tres Marías and came down with Roscoe to help us enjoy the day.

After one delicious Christmas dinner, the kids gave a program: plays, poems and songs. Forrest Cammack sang "How Great Thou Art", causing all to shed tears. Maybe we were a bit homesick.

"It was a good day, in spite of a two-hour council meeting," I wrote the folks in the north. "It seems we can never get together without talking shop. But the joy of fellowship, listening to Jack's jokes, laughing, and playing games, made Christmas special."

I longed to have a traditional Christmas but since that wasn't possible, I learned to adapt. We also learned some valuable lessons: we didn't need many gifts; inexpensive ones from the trunk would provide hours of fun; evergreen trees were not essential; red poinsettias provide Christmas color; even though the menu changed because of circumstances we could always make a festive meal with cranberries and olives brought from the States. Packages of mincemeat and candied fruit, made into pies and fruitcake, added that special touch.

The Aymaras taught us the most important lessons. Even though life was hard for some, they found the real meaning of the season in the Christmas story. Singing carols with them— "Silent Night", "Away In A Manger", and others, left us with a warm glow, thankful we could spend Christmas in Bolivia.

Kids swimming at Christmastime

Rocks, Machetes and Guns

Opposition to the Gospel and persecution of believers were not uncommon in the Yungas. In 1955, the year we moved to the Yungas to plant churches, an unwise missionary in southern Bolivia encouraged believers to take a religious image apart. In so doing they demonstrated that it was made only of plaster of paris. Thus it had no power. This act became national news.

Another event fueled this cauldron of heated debate. Two groups of believers met in Nogalani for midweek meetings and agreed to destroy their idols.

"Let's root out idolatry," yelled a zealous new believer. "Bring your idols to meeting next time. We want to get rid of all that displeases God."

The following week, believers brought everything that pertained to their former worship in the State church, and that which they had used in their animistic worship: *ekekos* (little household gods), sacred stones, *calaveras* (skulls used for placing curses on people), statues of the virgin Mary, various saints, crucifixes, and

155

many other items. They smashed them to pieces with rocks, piled them behind the Catholic church, then set fire to all that would burn.

As the believers sat singing in service afterwards, a very angry antiprotestant group stormed into the meeting room. The interlopers beat believers with whips and clubs, tore picture rolls from the walls to pile with Bibles and hymnals in the center of the room, then set fire to them.

Women shrieked. Everyone tried to escape. In the scuffle, a club killed a sleeping baby.

We were away from the Yungas at the time, so the brethren went to the police in Coripata, asking for an official document guaranteeing protection. Before we arrived home from La Paz, however, a missionary from another group arrived to help settle the problem.

"Please, may I see the document," he asked.

After reading it, he calmly lit a match, then set the paper ablaze.

"As believers, we do not depend upon the law, but upon God." he explained. "The use of the law is sin. We have to suffer sometimes, so be ready to suffer even unto death."

Those were hard words for new believers and most of them dropped away from the church.

"It's better not to be an evangelical if there is no protection from the law," they said. Fear gripped their hearts, making the entire area unproductive for evangelicals.

Sometimes we experienced more subtle forms of persecution.

"I hear it is our fault that people here in Pichu can't harvest their crops," Roscoe chatted with Berno one evening.

"Yes, the mudslide cut the cable that held the swinging bridge, so they can't cross the river to get their crops out," Berno explained.

"Believers get blamed for a lot of things," Roscoe added. "When the *sari* ate Anselmo's *yuca*, they said it was because he was a believer."

"Before the rains started, they blamed us for the drouth," I contributed from the kitchen. "Now that we have rain and lots of slides, that's our fault too."

"Well, our shoulders are broad. We can joke about being blamed for all misfortune, about being odd, about having tails and eating frogs, but this is no joking matter for the church in Arapata right now." Roscoe's frown showed great concern. "Yesterday they said another baby died of smallpox. That makes eight children from the community and Mama Zenovia from the church. Of course the community is blaming the church for all the deaths. We need to pray they will stand firm in their faith."

"Five children have died here in Pichu from scarlet fever," I said. "I expect we'll get blamed for this too."

"I understand that some who are opposed to the Gospel went to the altiplano for a witchdoctor," Berno added.

"Yes," Roscoe explained, "but their children died even though a witchdoctor came with all his remedies. None of the children who have been brought to us for medicine have died and no believer children have died. Thank the Lord!"

Even some in the government worked against the protestant church. When officials came down to Pichu from La Paz to settle a land dispute, they encouraged people to dynamite believers' homes.

"Why do you do what the missionary says? They're here just to rob the Bolivians. The government is going to expel all of them—going to send them to Santa Cruz to work as slaves, then who will you follow?"

157

"That's not true," someone argued. "They're here to help us. They've brought us the truth for the first time." A heated debate followed, but Pichu believers stood firm.

Until the adoption of the Agrarian Land Reform in 1952, all Bolivian farms operated under the old serf system, brought from Spain in the 1500s. Spanish nobles divided the land into large parcels, called *haciendas*. Aymaras living on the land became *peons* (serfs), property of the *hacienda*. Land owners forced them to work several days a week for the privilege of living on and farming a small acreage. They virtually became slaves of the landowner. Most owners lived in the city so they hired administrators to be in charge of all farming activity.

Catholicism came with serfdom and was forced upon the Aymara. They merely added it to their animistic religion. Centuries later, after accepting serfdom and the Catholic religion, the Aymaras suffered much opposition when they opted to become Protestants.

In Milluhuaya the administrator forced believers to work on Sunday so they couldn't attend services. He also insisted they pay their quota for community *fiestas*.

"Why should we have to pay for the alcohol, if we don't take part in the *fiesta*?" believers argued.

When they won that battle, the administrator accused them of disturbing the peace with singing at late night meetings. Roscoe finally brought calm to the situation by explaining that Bolivian law gave religious freedom.

Priests often told believers it would offend the "little Virgin" if they didn't come back to the mother church. They reinforced their teaching by urging parishioners to put pressure on evangelicals.

Faint light rays were creeping down the canyon walls when Lady, our collie, awakened us with wild barking.

Roscoe awakened from a sound sleep to reach for his clothes. Being aware of scorpions, he carefully emptied each shoe before putting it on, then hurried down stairs to greet believers from Huancapampa.

"Buenos días, hermanos. What brings you out so early?"

Angry and frightened, Gregorio answered. "Pastor, we have a problem. The neighbors broke into our house last night. They tore up my Bible and hymn book, broke other things in the house and insulted my wife. They also took Mariano to jail and will try him this morning."

After breakfast Roscoe and Berno drove to Chulumani to get a guarantee of protection for the believers.

The court room soon filled with interested onlookers. As they listened to the story, Roscoe and Berno could see that apparently a powerful anti-protestant had lied about believers, then paid the lieutenant-governor to force them off the farm and divide their land among other peons on the farm.

"Why are you taking Mariano's land from him?" Roscoe questioned more closely.

"Because he refuses to cooperate with others on the farm."

"In what way does he refuse to cooperate?"

"He won't cooperate with the Catholic religion, nor in our *fiestas.*"

Always prepared, Roscoe pulled a legal document from his pocket to talk hard and long, trying to convince the lieutenant governor that Bolivia gave religious freedom to evangelicals and a guarantee from persecution.

The lieutenant governor argued his point but Berno interrupted with a lengthy defense of the law. His defense, in terminology that convinced everyone, amazed Roscoe. He saw how God could use an illiterate man for His glory.

"Yes, the law is on the books," the official grudgingly admitted. Apparently we were the first to enforce its use.

Later Roscoe took the official to Huancapampa to explain the law to a large group of peons. In response, some tried to explain the situation, but in doing so, they merely clarified their intent to the believers.

"Everything will be fine if Mariano gives up this evangelical religion."

"We don't want Mariano on the farm for fear everyone will want to be Christian," another added.

After leaving Mariano at his house, the fellows followed the winding road up the valley. They agreed that Satan was fighting hard to keep his territory, but felt confident that God was greater and would be victor.

Satan also fought hard for Sirupaya, another community a few miles below us. There was no space for a tent in this community so we pitched it in a little nitch in the bank, where trucks usually stopped to load oranges and bananas. Passing trucks sent showers of dust on to the tent. Only a few people came to meetings because many opposed our being there, but we planted the Seed. Braulio and Candicha came to Christ, along with another neighbor lady. Persecution caused these three to grow strong in their faith.

"Thump! Clatter! Bang!" Rocks hit the tin roof while we sang hymns and taught the Scriptures in Braulio's house in the weeks that followed the tent meeting. Gun shots rang out across the roof as we prayed. Neighbors threatened these new believers.

"Braulio," someone called from the road above. "Here is a police order for you because you have embraced a new religion." A policeman delivered the order then marched Braulio off to Yanacachi. When we heard about it, Roscoe went up to get him out of jail.

A week or two later a Dutch priest walked the road with Braulio in front of his house, trying to convince him of the error of his beliefs.

"Why have you left your mother faith? Oh, Braulio," he pleaded, "don't you know you have grieved the virgin mother?" But Braulio stood firm in his newfound faith.

After arguing for two hours the priest turned to Braulio. "I see you are well founded in your new faith. It's a good thing. Stick with it."

Sometime later we heard a knock, so Roscoe went down to find Braulio holding his little daughter.

"She's sick. Please, pastor, do you have some medicine?"

"We're going out to La Paz tomorrow," Roscoe advised after examining her and finding nothing wrong. "Bring her up. We'll take her out to the doctor."

"She's dying of malnutrition," Dr. Marshal announced the next day.

We were stunned when we heard neighbors had stolen Braulio's corn crop, so that he and his family had nothing to eat. Our gifts of canned milk and other food were too late.

Early one morning I opened the door to Braulio's knock. "My little girl died. Do you have some nails; I must build a box."

"The community won't let us bury her in the cemetery because we're evangelicals," Braulio explained as we visited in their home later.

That afternoon we sang, prayed, and explained the importance of the resurrection of the saints. We buried her in the corner of their field, high on the mountain.

"I won't see her here anymore, but I'll see her in Heaven." Braulio's voice broke as he wiped away the tears.

Almost every church experienced some measure of opposition. Sometimes it was directed toward believers and other times toward the missionary. Huayrapata had more than its share of trouble. We visited regularly, leaving the Travelall along the road, then hiking up the trail to meet with Salustiano and his family. During meeting, people often pounded on the back of the house to distract the Bible study.

One day when Salustiano and Alejandra were in their field, neighbors broke into the house, taking all their clothes and bedding. They were blamed for every misfortune in the community. One beautiful Sunday morning Roscoe climbed the mountain path for a meeting. Two hours later he said good-bye and prepared to leave.

"May I carry your briefcase?" little seven-year-old Felix asked. The two started down the trail, engrossed in little-boy talk. The trail divided into a Y where most people took the smoother, right branch. For some unknown reason Roscoe took the left branch, down past the spring and some muddy, marshy places. He disappeared under the orange trees, ducked under banana leaves hanging over the narrow path, then brushed past elephant-ear-size *balusa* leaves on his way down. Felix followed close on his heels. Jumping off the bank to the road, Roscoe was soon on his way home in the Travelall.

As he sped up the dusty road, Felix heard shouting and arguing.

"How did that *gringo* get away?" An angry mob, carrying clubs, rocks, and machetes swarmed down the trail to stand in the road watching the dust disappear in the wind.

While hiding along the path, Felix realized his neighbors had planned to kill the missionary.

God must have caused us to go down that other path, he reasoned. *God protected him. That was a miracle.*

God protected more times than we realized. As Roscoe came home from Arapata one afternoon, a man, carrying a gun, stopped him along the road. He proved to be the Secretary General of Pararani.

"*Buenas tardes, Señor.*" His words were harsh and commanding. "I've stopped you to say we don't want evangelicals on our farm any more. Don't come back here again."

"I'm sorry, Sir, but we have believers here in Pararani," Roscoe answered cautiously but firmly. "This is their home, and they will continue to have meetings."

Lifting the gun a bit, as though to emphasize his point,   and with a defiant snarl, the Secretary General warned, "You know what happened in Nogalani, don't you?"

We knew what had happened in Nogalani, the village where believers had been attacked. However, the following Sunday our family climbed a rocky path along the edge of coca terraces to have services in Pararani. We realized that we were in full view of the whole community, but we trusted the Lord for protection.

Pararani was an intensely fanatical community, extremely antiprotestant. Community anger knew no bounds when several months earlier, Eusebio Quispe, a peon in the community, listened to the message of the Gospel at a street meeting in La Paz. He then went into the church to pray and find the Lord Jesus as Savior. Back in Pararani, his wife, Inéz, joined him in his enthusiasm for the Lord. None of his neighbors, however, would have anything to do with this new religion.

"Let's get rid of this guy," they plotted. The opportune moment came a short time later.

"Inéz, I'm going to town. I'll be home before dark." With that laconic announcement, Eusebio ducked under the banana leaves which hung over the path and was soon lost from sight in the growth around his house. He often walked the five kilometers to Coripata for kerosene, matches, or just to sit in the plaza and visit with his friends. Since he had become an evangelical he didn't have too many friends, but this day he was fortunate.

"*Buenas tardes, amigo.*"

"*Qué tal, hermano?* What's new today, brother?" Eusebio squatted in the shade of the large canopy of purple bougainvilla, where the two talked, oblivious to time. Hours passed. Dim street lights flickered on the plaza.

"Aye, it's late. I must go." Eusebio jumped to his feet. "I promised Inéz I would be back before dark. We'll talk another day. *Hasta luego.*"

He hurried down the cobblestone street, under the dim street lights, past open doorways through which candle light flickered, and out into the dark of the countryside.

"I shouldn't have stayed so late, for there is no moon tonight," he muttered to himself, as he trotted down the road, picking his way carefully along the white dusty truck tracks.

Early that afternoon neighbors had seen Eusebio hike down his path.

"He's probably going to town. Now's our chance." They gleefully plotted their strategy, joining the farm owner in a prearranged scheme.

"We'll meet on the cliff above the path, in the *chumi*, where the tall weeds hide the big rocks."

All arrived early to line the rocks in a handy position for rolling down the hill.

"Be sure to cover them with weeds and grass," the leader of the gang advised. "Make it look natural, so people will think they just accidently rolled down."

They waited—and waited. It got chilly so they wrapped their *mandils* around their shoulders.

"You can see the path better than I," someone whispered. "Give me a signal when to push."

"I'll let you know. Keep low."

Time passed.

"Are you sure you saw him go to town?"

"I'm sure," someone replied emphatically, not wanting to lose face.

Some dozed. Others filled their cheeks with coca leaves to ease the hunger pangs, then chewed to keep awake.

A *lechusa* hooted in a nearby tree, causing an anxious start for some.

"Oh, that's just an owl," another whispered with relief.

They chuckled at their own tenseness and soon settled down for a comfortable snooze, leaving one to watch the path below.

Eusebio hummed a tune as he followed the tracks. Dogs ran out to bark. Bats darted across the road. Justino urged his burro up the trail to his home in Tabacal. A *lechusa* swooped low over his head. *If I didn't know the Lord, I'd be afraid to be out here after nightfall. My father told of evil spirits lurking nearby at night. He always warned that we shouldn't be out by ourselves.*

His thoughts were interrupted as he crossed the bridge below the *hacienda* house.

Hmmm, everything is dark up there tonight. Must be gone.

Again he took up a tune to relieve the tension as he hurried through dark shadows—"What a Friend we Have in Jesus".

I haven't been on the old trail for a long time, he thought suddenly. *I think I'll go up that way tonight. It may be lighter too, since there is no moon.* Quietly passing the old farm house, he followed the trail through the community.

"Yoohoo, I'm home," he called as he crossed the slate-paved patio and ducked through the low door into the kitchen. Inéz sat sleepily knitting by the light of a rag wick in a small can of kerosene.

"Oh!" she started. "I'm glad you're home. It's quiet around here."

"Yes, I'm glad too. Let's go to bed. I'm tired."

They were soon sound asleep and only the dog curled by the door gave any sign of life. A growl now and then proved he was on guard and suspicious of activity nearby.

Sometime after midnight the stealthy neighbors awakened from their snooze.

"I'm going home. I don't think Eusebio went to town."

"Ow, I'm stiff from sitting in this position."

One by one they left.

The dog fell into a sound sleep, as he guarded the Quispe home.

The next day the neighbors heard Eusebio had arrived home by a circuitous route to sleep soundly all night. Some were angry. Others accused the leader for having given false information. Some made plans to try again. But a few began to wonder about Eusebio's God.

That occurance marked the turning point in Pararani. Eusebio's faithfulness through much persecution softened many hearts. When we arrived with the tent, several were converted, much to the consternation of the owner of the farm.

During the following months we often journeyed to Pararani for meetings. We usually drove in at the farm house and left our Travelall to hike up the trail about ten minutes to Eusebio's house, where sometimes as many as 40 believers gathered to study the Bible.

One Sunday when we parked, the farm house door suddenly flew open.

"You can't park your car here," the owner yelled. "It just causes fights between your believers and my peons. It's all your fault."

Roscoe got out to talk, but the owner was in no talking mood. Poking Roscoe in the chest, he raised his voice even more, yelling, "There's been some stealing around here, and your believers are the guilty ones."

"How do you know?" Roscoe asked. "We don't condone such actions. If it's true, they need to be punished."

"All these people are just ignorant Indians: liars, thieves." His heated accusations didn't set well with Roscoe, but he listened patiently. "You can't trust them. The only trustworthy one around here is Eusebio Quispe."

Roscoe smiled inwardly, wanting to say, "See, that's what the Gospel does," but he couldn't get a word in edgewise.

"We didn't have all this trouble until you came teaching not to respect the priest." Again he poked Roscoe in the chest with a long finger. "You teach them not to chew coca, so the price of coca is going down, and that's all your fault too. You also teach them not to mourn their dead so there are no more fiestas. Four of our officials here on my farm are believers now and that isn't good," he spat out emphatically, punctuating his words with a vigorous nod of his head.

"Remember, I told you several months ago, Bolivia does uphold religious freedom, so your people have a right to...."

He cut Roscoe's words short. "I know. I know that the country has religious freedom," he retorted angrily, "but that is just as long as it doesn't interfere with the Catholic religion." Then changing his tone abruptly, he asked, "By the way, what's your goal here, anyway?"

"I'm here to preach the Gospel, to tell people about Jesus: how He can forgive their sins and change their lives, how He can bring peace where there is so much strife."

Abruptly the owner interrupted and demanded, "I want a joint meeting of Catholics, Protestants, authorities, my priest and you."

"No," Roscoe flatly refused. "There would only be a fight and nothing would be accomplished." But thinking to pacify the owner, he added, "I'll talk to the believers to see what they want."

"What does it matter what they think?" the owner exploded again. "Are you on the same level with them? Aren't you better than they? They don't have any rights nor any say about it."

Knowing the argument could never be settled, Roscoe nodded to the family, then picked up his briefcase to leave.

"Wait a minute, who's going to answer for all the trouble around here?"

"The guilty should be punished," Roscoe calmly responded. "As for us and the believers, we'll ask God for solutions."

"Aw, God's up in Heaven," the owner retorted. "He doesn't have anything to do with us down here."

We went on up the trail to the service confident that God was in control and expecting to see the Pararani church grow under persecution. It did. But with the persecution came the need for much training so they could stand firm in their faith.

Persecuted family by home in Yungas

On Down the Trail

Yungas Bible School

With many churches, only two pastors, and no trained workers, by 1957 we were desperate. Sixteen young fellows went to Copajira Bible School on the high plains, but eleven swung their packs on their backs and came back to the Yungas the first month.

Lord, what do we do? We can't pastor all these places. Neither is it right that we do so. Help!

We took our concern to the mission council. Every month the council met, either at the farm or in La Paz, to conduct mission business. We discussed such things as farm problems, Bible School, general field reports of growth and problems. After sharing our concerns about the Yungas work and lack of workers, a long discussion followed:

"Maybe it would be better to pay pastors; then we wouldn't lack workers."

"I'm against paying pastors. It would be better to appoint elders to lead."

"I'm in favor of paying if there is no other way."

"Local churches should take responsiblity for supporting their pastors. It's not good to use foreign funds for this purpose."

"Frankly, I think pastors should be consecrated enough to work without pay. After all, they are working for the Lord."

"How deep would our consecration be if we didn't receive our $90.00 each month and we had no savings, no money for clothes, travel and other essentials?"

"One thing is certain—what we decide for the Yungas must also be practiced here on the altiplano. Our entire national church will be affected by our decision on this matter."

We all agreed that the elder system would work best until the Aymara church grew large enough to support its own work.

Back in the Yungas, our concern for the work weighed heavily on the entire family. Even the children felt our burden for the situation and joined us in prayer during family devotions. Sometimes their prayers were more to the point: "Lord, please help us have lots of big churches here in the Yungas." After a long pause, Beverly added, "and lots of people in 'em."

Often we discussed the pros and cons of the matter. On one such occasion Roscoe tossed out his analysis of the situation.

"The Lord is making a few things very clear to me. We asked Him for pastors. He sent them, but they didn't stay. Nine young pastors came from the altiplano. Each contributed to the work but it was either too far from home, too hot, too many biting insects, sickness, or wives who refused to go with their husbands. Whatever the reason, they came and they went, deciding that pastoral work here in the Yungas wasn't for them. Perhaps

God gave to us because we kept asking, but all the time He knew that we shouldn't have them."

"How could that be? Do you mean that God doesn't want us to have pastors?" I argued. "That's not Biblical."

"Yes, He wants us to have pastors. Look, several young fellows have gone to Copajira to Bible School, but they can't adjust to the cold climate up there, so how can we expect altiplano graduates to serve as pastors in the Yungas."

"Uh-huh," I nodded. "It sounds logical."

"Maybe God has another method of pastoring these Yungas churches." Roscoe shrugged his shoulders, then turned palms up to show a complete surrender of the problem. "However He wants to do it is okay with me. Anyway, we've learned our lesson. If God says 'no,' He must have another way of solving the problem."

A little later the Lord dropped an idea into our minds.

"Let's start a Yungas Bible School—a school for laymen, to train workers."

"Roscoe, are you sure that your idea is from the Lord? Do you realize that we have meetings almost every night? We have no classrooms, no dormitory, no kitchen, no nothing for a Bible School." I gesticulated with my hands to emphasize my point.

"I know...the idea sounds crazy, but we could use the little army tent for a classroom—we only have to have one room. And we can use the garage for a dorm."

"They could sleep in the guestroom up above the garage," I added, becoming excited about the idea.

"The kitchen would be no problem for them, as long as it doesn't rain."

"It sounds like *your* problems are solved, but I have a few questions. Who's going to teach? How long are we going to have classes? What about books? Who is going to teach *our* kids?" I went off to the kitchen to fix a bite to eat, leaving him to put his ideas on paper.

Action began immediately. "Berno, the little army tent is full of holes. If it rains we'll have a problem."

"That's no problem at all," Berno responded without a second thought. "Just cover the holes with wax." So we melted candles then poured the wax over the tent. Presto! A classroom. Dried banana leaves on the floor served as mattresses and made our guest room and garage into fine dorm rooms. On three sides of his house, Berno built lean-tos of bamboo poles with banana leaf thatch. Students would use them for cooking and storing dry wood.

"How many students can we accomodate, Berno?" Roscoe asked as we surveyed our accomplishments.

"About thirty."

"Ha-ha," I laughed. "If thirty squeeze into that space, they won't be able to turn over for fear someone will get squashed." Shaking my head I skipped down the steps to see how the Knight students were doing. *Incredible!* I thought. *This place was built for a rest cabin. Whoever thought it would house a Bible School for 30 students?*

But it did. The first Yungas Bible School opened March 11, 1957. For two weeks it was a busy, busy place.

Fearful that we would be caught unprepared, we made a hasty trip to La Paz for 500 sheets of study helps, which we ran off on the duplicator. We also bought supplies for a store so students could buy food they needed—100-pound sacks of potatoes, pasta, rice, flour and sugar; a whole carcass of mutton jerky, cans of sardines, boxes of matches, bars of soap, round molds of chocolate and smaller amounts of chili peppers and salt.

Students brought their own bedding, soup bowl, spoon, cooking pot, *chuños* and green bananas, money to buy what they needed at a reduced price, and willing hearts to learn. We wanted the Yungas work to be wholly indigenous, so the students took care of their own expenses.

"Well, the classes were a complete success---much better than we expected," I wrote to our folks in the north two weeks later.

Thirty-five students enrolled and 26 of these were here full time. Several could neither read nor write, but have been memorizing texts and learning by osmosis. We taught several classes: Life of Christ, Old Testament History, Bible Synthesis, Doctrine, How to Conduct Services, Texts, Illustrated Evangelism, Music, and Reading (for those who can't read). With chapel every morning and meeting every n i g h t, we had a long day—from 8 a.m. till 10 p.m.

Roscoe taught in Aymara, and they loved it. When he lacked a word they gladly filled in, so he is learning along with them. One time he meant to say 'He sweat drops of blood' but he said 'drops of frogs'. Of course everyone roared.

I had to use an interpreter, but all went smoothly except for the time the interpreter didn't want to say that Jacob had children by four wives. He was fearful the new believers would think it okay to have many wives. Such bits of scripture have to be explained.

Even your grandchildren are learning in these classes. Last evening we were discussing the events of the day. "Daddy, are we all saints?" Gary asked.

Before Roscoe could utter a sound, Karen piped up, "No, our family's not."

We exploded with laughter. Karen never wastes time offering her opinions, and they usually cause an uproar.

The brethren were happy to learn so many hymns and choruses, but I've about lost my voice. At meeting each night we sang for an hour.

Sunday was a big day: singing, Sunday School, more singing, preaching, altar service, testimonies, and more singing. A flannelgraph lesson resulted in another altar service with two new converts giving their testimonies afterwards. They followed this with a healing service and more singing. Finally, after Roscoe used the lantern projector to show slides, they finished the day with more singing.

"I'm sure the Yungas Bible School will produce good fruit for years to come," Roscoe commented as we dropped into bed that night. "These two weeks we've stressed what Dawson Trotman taught: 'That which you know, teach to another.' These 35 men are our future evangelists, pastors, Sunday School teachers, the backbone of the work." We drifted off to sleep with visions of a thriving Yungas church.

Next morning I watched as the Travelall slowly pulled out of the yard and up the mountain road. With students waving from every window and strains of "God Be With You" floating back across the morning air, I realized the first Yungas Bible School was history.

"Mommie, why are you crying?" Karen asked as I wiped away the tears.

"Just because I'm happy, honey. Someday you'll understand." I gave her a hug as we hurried down to start school for the day. 176

"Just because I'm happy, honey. Someday you'll understand." I gave her a hug as we hurried down to start school for the day.

After the success and enthusiasm of the first Yungas Bible School, it grew to be a twice-a-year event. By 1959, 73 men from 20 churches attended. Other missionaries helped teach at various times, and national graduates of the altiplano Bible School made a great addition to our teaching staff.

"These classes are proving to be the making of our Yungas pastors," I wrote to friends in the north. "They require patience, simplicity, time and strength, but are well worth the effort."

Classes were not over yet when husbands began asking for classes for their wives. Realizing that their success rested upon the support of their wives, they begged for "just one week". We read between the lines, knowing the men could not care for their homes and fields alone.

The following year word spread up and down the valleys: *Women's Bible School* for one week! It was a challenge to teach Bible to 31 Aymara women. Only three could read, write or speak Spanish, but the Holy Spirit taught them. These classes became a yearly event and attendance grew from 31 to 70 women, plus 25 babies and small children by 1959. They overflowed our dorm, garage, guest room and, finally, we used the old army tent for latecomers. They came on trucks. They came on foot. All carried packs on their backs: kettles, soup bowls, blankets, green bananas, Bibles, hymnals, and some with babies. It was amazing how they could adjust a baby on top of all that pack!

Two women walked two long days up the mountain, each carrying a large pack and one with a baby in her arms.

"We want to learn, but we don't have any money, so we walked," they explained. They walked 30 miles up a mountain—always up—in the rain, to study the Bible for one week!

As I taught the women I kept seeing flashes of color—young children and babies playing with flowers. Suddenly I realized mothers were picking my flowers for their children—hibiscus, sweet-smelling gardenia, orange nasturtiums, pink tea roses from the corner of the veranda and the prolific impatiens. Invariably, in just a short time petals were strewn on the ground and forgotten. This upset me. Flowers were my pride and joy. They picked my flowers just to destroy them. I resented that. Then I remembered a lesson I thought I'd learned while living at the farm a few years before. When women came into the patio, they often either sat on my flowers or picked them. I grumbled.

"Let me tell you of my experience in Guatemala," Julia Pearson, a fellow missionary, counseled. "When the maid broke my prized teapot, R. Esther Smith (another fellow missionary) found me in tears. After listening to my story, she looked straight at me and said, 'Julia, thee will have to remember that souls are more precious than dishes'."

So the Lord spoke to me. "Thee will have to remember, Tina, that souls are more precious than flowers."

I dried my tears and tried to remember that flowers would bloom again, hopefully in the hearts of Aymara women.

Bible class

Students cooking at Bible School

Yungas Bible School

Growth

Excitement ran high when the churches organized. It gave the brethren a sense of belonging to something official, important and permanent. Like us, they desired an indigenous work—self-governing, self-supporting, and self-propagating.   They chose their own presidents, secretaries and treasurers who were responsible for teaching the Sunday School lesson, calling the roll and keeping records. Adults and children met together for two hours or more of singing, discussing the lesson, and prayer. Everyone knelt to pray aloud, all at the same time. This was their routine for every service—two on Sunday and two during the week.

For centuries Aymaras have celebrated special days with *fiestas*. These special days, sometimes lasting a full week, become times of debauchery, with much drinking, dancing, fighting and immorality. As people became believers, the church provided a ready substitute for their *fiestas* in the form of quarterly meetings, yearly meetings and conferences.

A great sense of accomplishment pervaded the church when officials and pastors from La Paz met with 115 Yungas brethren at Pararani for the first quarterly business meeting. The impressive service for installing officers thrilled these believers, less than a year old spiritually. Now they were a part of a larger organization.

"When you have problems don't go to Don Raúl," Carmelo, the Yearly Meeting president advised. "Come to us."

Roscoe felt the barb of that statement, for, after all, weren't these our spiritual children? Then he realized the truth of the statement.

"This is what we have been working toward," he said. "It is an indigenous church, and they should be in control."

We searched for ways to keep enthusiasm high. "The churches need to interact with each other. They need to know each other better. How about having a Conference?" Roscoe suggested.

We held our first Yungas Conference in Chacala. It set a precedent for the yearly conferences that followed.

"Roscoe, you remember that Niconor's patio is just big enough for the little army tent. There isn't room for anything larger," I warned.

"We'll make room."

I envisioned them cutting down prized hibiscus or bougainvillea. But the patio was just large enough, although the tent covered one cotton plant and two coffee trees. These provided the aesthetic touch for services.

Conference day started early. At 5:00 a.m. a rooster crowed, a donkey brayed, and someone started praying aloud. All joined in the morning prayers before climbing out of their blankets. By six o'clock most of the men had seated themselves in the tent for morning vespers. Women weren't excluded; some attended, but most had other important duties to perform.

They chatted at the spring where many sat on tufts of grass, combing and braiding their long, black hair. Some washed their dusty feet and legs under a trickle of water from a banana *chala*. Others dipped water with their hands to rub over bare-bottomed babies, before carefully wrapping them tightly in ribbons of cloth, after which they folded them into many-colored *ahuayos* then swung them up onto their backs. This morning ritual prepared them for the day.

A few women had no time to visit at the spring. They chatted, however, as they coaxed a wood fire to boil the husks of the coffee bean for that daily breakfast of *sultana*, and *mariqueta*, a hard French roll. The latest gossip passed around the circle as women peeled potatoes or husked green bananas, preparing for the noon meal. One woman in a dark corner of the kitchen missed all the gossip. She ground red chile pods and cumin on the rock mortar on the floor. The slap-slap of rock on rock wasn't conducive to chit-chat.

A carcass of jerky, vying for space with smoke garlands, hung from the rafters, waiting to be hacked in pieces for the soup. Below, someone cleaned rice, being careful to pick out the tell-tale signs of little creatures, such as mice or cockroaches, that invaded the kitchen. Red coals glowed under pots of boiling *chuños*, bananas, *yuca*, soup and rice. It was a busy place when I poked my head in the door.

"*Hermana*, teach us a class," they begged.

How could I refuse? I carried flannelgraph figures, puppets, or flashcards for just such opportunities, knowing that the women in the kitchen missed all the classes of the day.

Evangelists came from La Paz to speak to the conference. Pablo's class on Daniel and Revelation captivated everyone with his large banners of Nebuchadnezzar and the beasts prancing across the front of the tent. Everyone loved to sing and delighted in learning new hymns and choruses. Believers soaked up new teaching like sponges.

One hundred forty brethren, five of them having walked 25 miles, spent three wonderful days at the first Yungas Conference. The next year 200 from 14 churches attended the yearly conference held at Anacu. We Knights slept in the Travelall and ate with the brethren. The conference offered a spiritual feast for all with no distractions aside from a few rain showers and a jillion biting flies.

Another year the family and several brethren loaded for a third conference, but we got only as far as the bridge where a mudslide blocked the road. Roscoe and the brethren walked four hours on to Pararani, carrying their packs, briefcase, box of Bibles and hymnals and the medical kit, while the kids and I took the Travelall back home.

Conferences became the highlights of the year and gave us confidence that God was answering our prayer of faith. However, along with exciting highs came lows when discouragement tempted us.

Sometimes capable leaders turned back to the world, preferring their *fiestas* of the former life. Some became fearful when their families turned against them. Others couldn't stand in the face of persecution.

At one low point we reminded ourselves that growth does not come without effort and sometimes disappointment. Neither is it measured only in numbers.

"Even Jesus didn't convince everyone," Roscoe encouraged me. "He lost many."

We tried to be optimistic, to focus on growth, not the negative. Growth meant watching Benancio and his wife kneel before each other at the front of the church to ask pardon. Then they left their tithe of a rooster with legs tied, and testified of God's dealings in their lives.

"Division means growth sometimes too, even though we don't like it," Roscoe explained. "Tabacal wants its own meeting, so those believers have pulled out of Pararani. But that means one more church."

However, when growth becomes an obsession it can become a dangerous temptation. We seriously studied the offer to take another demonination's group into our work.

"No, I can't build on another's foundation," Roscoe decided. "We'll just continue to plant the Seed, to disciple and to lift up the fallen."

"The Helen Ross Memorial church at Mina Chojlla has almost folded," he reported to the mission board. "The mine laid off 800 of its 1000 workers so the church is bare. Only two men plus a few women and children remain, and they aren't too faithful. The pastor left also, so we must start from scratch to rebuild. I'm sure God opened the door for us in that place so surely He won't let the devil close it now."

"The work at Mina Chojlla is reviving," we reported the following year. "It looked hopeless but today the future is bright and the work is growing. A worker walks from Anacu every week, from ten miles down the river, to have services with them. Tomás receives no pay, goes faithfully, and is doing a good job."

Other churches grew also. "Pichu is growing," Berno reported one Sunday evening. "They appointed two women to visit all the women of the community to invite them to service."

As a result of this action, women of the church began to meet Tuesday mornings for prayer. During one of their prayer times the Lord guided them to bring encouragement to the missionary.

It was a dark, dreary day and pouring rain—as it had been for several days. Boulders tumbled in the roaring river below. Dark clouds hung low over the canyon. Mudslides stopped traffic. Gary and Beverly wrote compositions while I helped Karen with her reading. Lady barked. Gary peeked out his upstairs bedroom window.

"Mommie, the little woman is here."

"On a day like this?" I exclaimed, as I went downstairs.

I opened the door to find, standing under the eaves, the most drenched person I'd seen in a long time.

"*Buenos días, hermana,*" Genoveva greeted me cheerfully.

"Genoveva, do come in. Come in out of this terrible weather." I swung the door wider to pull her inside. Before I could do so, she removed her dripping derby hat and put it on the rocks outside the door, not wanting to get my floor wet.

After retrieving the hat, I invited her to sit down. Being short in stature and not being accustomed to sitting on chairs, she swung the pack from her back, placed it on the floor, then sat beside it.

"I've come to visit you, *hermana.*"

So we visited. We talked of the weather, of their crops, of the slides and finally touched on the brethren at the church. She reported growth in the lives of some.

"I'm glad you came. I've been lonely," I confessed.

"That's the reason I came," she explained. "You see, this morning we met for prayer as usual. We prayed for you, and we prayed for pastor Raúl. There were only three of us, but after prayer, we felt that someone should come down to see if you needed anything. We knew pastor Raúl was in Chile, and you've been alone for two weeks. We thought maybe you might need some food."

Genoveva opened her *bulto* then handed me a squash, a few ears of corn and some *yuca*.

I was touched and could hardly find words to thank her so I hugged her.

"Thank you so much for coming," I mumbled with a husky voice.

"I must be going." Genoveva picked up her empty colorful *ahuayo*, swung it onto her back, pulled her hat down low over her eyes and went out the door.

"*Hasta luego* (until later)," she called.

Through tears I watched her disappear up the road— lost in the rain. God sent her just when I needed her.

Evangelizing

Temporary meeting place

Tested

"*Señor* Raúl Nait,

.....there are now 20 new believers meeting every week. We need Bibles and hymnals. We also would like for you to visit us so we can learn more about this new religion......"

signed with several signatures and
two thumb prints

"Praise the Lord for new believers!" Roscoe announced as he handed me the crumpled sheet of notebook paper, folded to make an envelope. Someone had passed it on via the unorthodox Yungas postal system. "That means one more group meeting and 20 more believers."

"God is going to have to work fast if there are a thousand believers in our churches before furlough time," I commented.

"Yes. Growth doesn't come without effort, however, so tomorrow we'll visit farms and communities in North Yungas."

Early next morning Berno and Roscoe left, picked up two believers from Chacala, then spent the day evangelizing. Going in pairs, they visited house to house, leaving tracts and a Gospel of John. That night they curled up in the Travelall to sleep.

Next day they evangelized in South Yungas, passing out tracts and trying to arrange for tent meetings.

With both missionaries and nationals spending many hours in personal evangelism, tent meetings, discipling, teaching Bible School classes, and encouraging established churches, the work grew. Roscoe wrote to his dad:

> We're going to be busy with classes the next few weeks. It's a necessity for our people, for we now have 27 groups meeting and only three pastors. But the Holy Spirit is their pastor. Don't forget to pray for the thousand souls we've asked of the Lord. We have a long way to go in a short time, but I still have faith that God will answer. This is the greatest test of my life, but I will come out victorious.

We prayed constantly for entire families. In a culture where the wife often carries the spiritual load, Roscoe contacted the man, feeling that if they were converted, wives and children would follow. This often proved true, but not always.

Filomena faithfully walked with the Lord—Victor couldn't leave his drink. Adela attended services— Ponciano preferred politics. Some wives attended service while their husbands played soccer every Sunday morning. Other men wanted to "believe" after they celebrated their annual fiesta.

Furlough approached quickly.

"Why hasn't God answered?" Roscoe's frown showed his disappointment.

"God may not be interested in the number of churches or buildings but He IS interested in souls being saved," I tried to encourage him. "If `God is not willing that any should perish' is still true, it surely means He has heard."

We clung to God's promises.

"...my Word...shall not return unto me void."

"...there hath not failed one word of all His good promise...."

"...they that sow in tears shall reap in joy..."

Still doubt crept in.

How could God fail? Roscoe spent hours on his knees in the prayer room reading the Word and pouring out his hurt and disappointment. "Why is it, Lord, that you worked miracles for Mueller and Goforth and Taylor? Why did you answer their prayers and not mine? Why, Lord? Where do I lack? Show me," he pleaded.

Even the children sensed our concern for the work. "What's wrong with daddy?" Gary asked one evening. "He doesn't laugh anymore."

Discouragement had taken its toll until even the family felt its effects. Physical tiredness, resulting from days of evangelizing and many nights of meetings affected his emotions.

"Well, I'm through," Roscoe announced one evening after a long hard day. "The Lord will have to do the rest."

We reached the bottom emotionally. Then little by little we began to emerge from that perplexing time of darkness and despair. Every morning as I gazed up the ravine where my mountain peak glowed with a halo of early morning light, I was reminded of God's faithfulness. He was more steadfast and faithful than that mountain. We *could* trust His Word: "I will not leave you nor forsake you."

God didn't forsake us. At last the day came when Roscoe came down from the prayer room with a sparkle in his eyes.

"Listen to this, honey. I've found my answer in Job this morning. 'Though He slay me, yet will I trust Him.' I don't know why He didn't give us a thousand souls; but regardless, I trust Him."

We felt as though we had come out of a dark tunnel. We shed tears together and made plans for furlough. Seven hundred believers, 27 groups and ten church buildings sent us on our way to the States to tell the story of the Yungas.

Furlough should bring excitement for missionary families. It's a time to relax from the pressures of the work—a time to share our successes and failures, to unload our frustrations. It's a time to visit family—to let grandparents spoil their grandchildren. Furlough means a time to fellowship with friends—to visit churches and hear them promise to pray for us another term. It's a time for new foods, for drinking water from the tap, for not having to mix powdered milk every night, for eating vegetables that haven't been soaked in disinfectant. It's a time to tell about the victories won and battles lost on the field. It's a different life from that experienced on the mission field.

As our furlough year drew near, the kids didn't want to leave their beloved Yungas. Roscoe and I were in agreement. We had no enthusiasm for leaving either.

Instead, we felt a heavy burden for the work and a knot of fear gripped our hearts. It wasn't the furlough time itself that we feared, for we had many stories to tell of victories won by Aymaras in the Yungas. But we felt concern for the brethren we would leave behind.

Who is going to take our place while we're home? Who will shepherd these new flocks, these new babes? Who will teach them?

As we struggled with our fears and the mission board struggled with choosing a couple to take our place, the Lord spoke a comforting word.

"Look what the Lord says to us," Roscoe announced one morning as he came into the kitchen. "'You have not chosen me, but I have chosen you, and ordained you, that ye should go and bring forth fruit, and that your fruit should remain...' Our fruit shall remain."

I wiped my hands. We talked and cried.

"It's God's promise to us, and we'll claim it. *He* will keep these new believers," Roscoe's tone of voice emphasized his faith. I saw months of concern roll off his shoulders.

A few weeks later word came from the north that David and Florence Thomas would come to the Yungas while we were on furlough.

"It's a comfort to leave the work in the Lord's hands, for, after all, it is His church." I breathed a sign of relief. "But the human in me makes me glad that Dave and Florence will be here."

"Yes, I'm glad they're coming, but I'm reminded that we must trust the Lord as though everything depended on *Him*, yet work as though everything depended on *us*. It's easy to say the work is the Lord's, then He gets the blame if it falls apart. It's not our fault." Roscoe rose to leave. "But sometimes through negligence or laziness we have to accept much of the blame."

"Where are you going?"

"I'm going out to grease the car for the next trip."

Roscoe came into this world with more adventure genes than most people, so when Leland and Iverna Hibbs came down for vacation, we talked about what lay beyond the mountains, down Caranavi way.

"I got a letter from some brethren in Santa Fe," Roscoe announced during the conversation. "They want a visit. How about going with me, Leland? I want to see what that area looks like."

Promptly they made plans for the trip. A few days later the Hibbs family arrived back in the Yungas. Early the next morning nine adult men and two missionary boys, Gary and Carol, loaded the Travelall for the trip to Caranavi.

"You said you didn't want to carry a load so here's your food. I hope it's enough. It's just packaged soup and a little dried fruit for nibbles." I handed it to Roscoe to be packed in with the men.

"Don't worry. We'll buy from people or I may have to kill a rooster." We both laughed as we remembered the true story of the miner who couldn't buy food along the trail so shot a chicken, then offered to pay for it.

"Don't forget to pay for it," I laughingly hollered, as they drove away.

That night they cooked packaged soup, then slept at the end of the road, along with cat skinners and others from the road crew.

"Let's get going, fellows," Roscoe aroused them at dawn. "We don't have any idea how long it will take us to get there."

Single file they started down a muddy trail. Dark clouds forecast the weather. It poured rain all day. They plodded on.....up the mountain, then down again, following the river, sometimes far below, other times fording it.

"I'm going to wear my shoes. They couldn't get any wetter," Leland announced as he plunged into the river. Others carried their shoes and hobbled across the river rocks. The Aymaras tied their shoes and pants in a bundle on their backs. As for Gary and Carol, they threw modesty to the wind; stripped stark naked, they braved the current.

The rivers flowed fast and deep, up to Gary's armpits, so he couldn't stand, but Berno saved the day. Grabbing his hand, they cautiously crossed the swift water with Gary floating out behind like a battered raft.

"There is no use putting on my clothes again," someone complained, "for we'll just have to cross another river soon." And they did. Three of them.

They grew tired of slopping down the muddy trail. They were starved, for they found no one living along the trail, no place to buy something to eat. Wood was soaked so they couldn't light a fire to cook their soup. After 13 long hours they straggled into Caranavi, only a few bamboo huts on the junction of two rivers. Under a leaky thatched roof, they rolled up in their sleeping bags and soon fell fast asleep from exhaustion, refusing to acknowledge the pangs of hunger.

At the crack of dawn they hit the trail again. Flocks of green parakeets twittered their way from tree to tree. Wild turkey and red-headed, green Amazon parrots left their roosts to find a breakfast of wild fruit. Iridescent blue butterflies fluttered among the tree-fern. While enjoying the beauty, the fellows scratched their fruit-fly bites and swatted at *távanos*, those pesky deer flies.

At the end of a long hard trip believers welcomed them warmly, showering them with gifts of cooking bananas, tomatoes, *yuca* and eggs. A helpful Aymara mama offered to cook these for their long trek out.

"What did you find?" I inquired when they got back home.

"We found 23 believers who are homesteading. They want the mission to build a church building and a school for them," Roscoe explained. "They also want us to pay for a school teacher."

"And?" I encouraged.

"I explained that we work on an indigenous system so if they come with us, they'll have to build their own church building and school house. They are of the old paternalistic system—many from our church in LaPaz —so they think the mission should provide everything. I encouraged them to carry on alone, as they have been doing for the past few years.

"Then your trip was all in vain?"

"No, some day we'll have a work in Caranavi area, but we'll wait for God's timing."

Several months later it seemed there were no more open doors for church planting in the Yungas.

"I wonder what the Lord's trying to tell us," Roscoe analyzed the situation. "It's dry season. We should be in tent meetings, but there are no calls for meetings."

Lord, you've promised to direct our paths. Which way, Lord, which way?

"Could it be that God is closing the Yungas so we'll start work in the Caranavi area?" Roscoe wondered aloud. "It's been three months since we made that trip on foot. They say the new road is finished now, so we could drive clear to Caranavi."

I felt dubious. "How can we take care of a work down there with follow-up? Discipling? It's a long way from home."

"Yes, it's about an eight-hour trip but if God is in this, He will provide a way," my optimistic husband encouraged me. Not too many weeks later we stood on the ridge at Chuspipata. Folds of purple mountains were lost in the distance. At our feet the precipice dropped into a deep, dim, dark green gorge, ending in a mysterious darkness of nothing. Here the narrow track of winding road clung to the cliff while winding through clouds of fog. Here the government had pushed political prisoners over the precipice. And from here we followed God's leading into the hot, humid Caranavi area.

We pitched the tent on a sandy beach. Maria and her ten-year-old son, Ceferino, were the only ones converted in that tent campaign. Furlough time aproached quickly and we feared for these two new believers. They had no one to teach them and lived far from other believers. Nevertheless, they were the seed that sprouted and years later produced a harvest of souls in Caranavi area.

It Shall Remain

"A trip to the Holy Land?" I asked.

"Yes, we've been saving our pennies a long time," Roscoe answered. "Now's the time to go. We'll take what the mission board gives us for the trip straight home, add our bit to it, and spend some time in Palestine."

"We don't want to go," the kids cried in unison. "We're tired of travel."

"How about spending the summer on the farm in Kansas?" I asked. "Grandpa Patterson would love to have you."

"Yeah! Yeah!"

"How will we get there?" Only Karen had doubts since she didn't remember the farm or Grandpa.

"We'll send you home on the plane," Roscoe explained. "Grandpa will meet you in Wichita."

They danced off up stairs, excited with the prospects of a summer on the farm. As for me, I had a few doubts about sending young children off by themselves.

The clear blue sky of the altiplano chased away any fears of a bumpy flight as we settled Gary, Beverly and Karen into their assigned seats on the Braniff plane bound for Dallas. We went early so they could become accustomed to the plane before we had to get off. When the time came, we gave quick hugs and the girls began to cry. Gary, carrying their Passport and responsible for his two sisters, tried to be brave.

A young man in uniform spoke from the seat behind. "Don't worry, Lady, the Marines will take care of them." We nodded thanks, then ducked out the door and down the steps. After watching the plane disappear into the west, we drove to the farm for a council meeting.

Back in La Paz we picked up a cable which read, "Kids arrived safe. Freeman". I breathed a sigh of relief.

After a three-month trip through Africa, Israel and Europe, nine months of meetings in the northwest and an ocean liner trip back to Bolivia, our little home in the Yungas canyon never looked better to us. We were home!

We were welcomed by the roar of the river, flocks of green parakeets chattering across the sky, our pets Cinders, Susie, and Sammy. Berno, who had faithfully carried on in our absence, greeted us.

"Tell us about it, Berno. How's the church doing? Are there new believers?"

"Fine, pastor. Everything is fine," came his laconic reply. Word spread fast throughout the Yungas that Don Raúl was back and soon pleas for visits filled our schedule. A two-hour hike up the mountain found Ilumaya faithful with meetings but with serious problems among the brethren. In another area an epidemic of whooping cough traveled from community to community. Several chronic tuberculosis patients were nearing their last days on earth and demanded our attention. Obviously everything wasn't fine, as Berno had said. But there were bright spots in the picture. At Huancané 300 people had squeezed into their new building for the Christmas program, and at least 200 went home for lack of space, so they said. The Yarija church, which had struggled for years, had suddenly come alive while we were gone, so they were enlarging their facilities. Arapata had two new daughter churches; Llojeta had two new outposts.

Every church showered us with flowers and fruit— whole heads of bananas, huge papayas, and sacks of oranges and tangerines.

We felt loved. The growth and enthusiasm we saw thrilled us. We rejoiced to see the Lord had been true to His promise, "I sent you to reap a harvest that *shall remain.*"

But problems had arisen while we were gone. Satan had tested the brethren by temptation from other denominations and cults. We called them wolves in sheep's clothing. Coripata church didn't like these strange doctrines so refused to leave our church.

"You are just a poor church," a pastor from another group told Berno. "The mission doesn't pay your pastors; you have to pay your own teachers and build your own churches. *Pobrecitos* (poor little ones). Come with us, and you will belong to a rich mission. We won't abandon you like Raúl has."

"Where does your money come from?" Berno asked. "What will happen to your church when that money is cut off from the north?"

"That day will never come," he arrogantly replied.

We listened as Berno recounted the struggle some churches had with this offer. We remembered the Sunday morning a missionary from another group had a service with one of our churches then offered tin roofing for their church building as an enticement to join his church, but the brethren refused it.

"How did they react to the arrogant offer of belonging to a rich mission?" we asked.

"They decided they would rather be proud of being a national church that didn't have to depend on others for support."

"Thank you, Lord," we silently prayed.

The work spread on down the river, up into other canyons and mountainsides, into new homesteading areas, on beyond to the end of the road. We either followed a trail or blazed one.

Steep palm-thatched roofs on bamboo walls became the national church trademark, as new churches followed homesteaders into the Caranavi area. Pascual and Mariano, young men who had studied at Copajira and the Yungas Bible School cleared jungle to establish homes and pastor churches.

Rafael, a former coca grower in south Yungas planted mangos on his terraces, which became a good source of income. With some of what God had given, he bought a motorcycle to evangelize.

"Juan, come with me. Let's evangelize down river."

The two men, carrying a box of literature and a small public address system, planted churches down the valley. This meant making trips to disciple new believers. Charoplaya, a result of their efforts, wanted its first Christmas program.

"I'll come down to help you with the program," Juan offered. "I'll be here early on Christmas eve."

Unfortunately, pouring rain brought a mud slide down the mountain to cut the road. When the truck could go no farther, Juan climbed down, paid his fare, and listened to the roar of the truck echoing up the canyon. He was alone. It was almost dark.

Spotting a *kayaco* tree, he cut a large umbrella leaf, then hunted for a walking stick. Swinging his pack on to his back and holding the *kayaco* leaf over his head to shield him from the rain, he gingerly felt his way across the moving, oozing mud with the walking stick, being careful not to get too close to the precipice. He walked seven miles on into the night to keep his promise he had made to new believers, a promise to teach them the real meaning of Christmas.

Nine consecutive weeks of meetings for Roscoe and Berno produced new fruit and encouraged established churches. Calls for meetings came from all across the field. We held some in almost inaccessible places.

One of these places was Marquirivi. The men drove to the end of the road at the river's edge, then loaded the tent equipment on to mules. Crossing a swinging footbridge, they climbed the mountain to start a new church.

"That bridge has an interesting story to tell," a muleteer explained as they hiked up the trail. "They have tried to build a bridge several times, but it always washes out. Some people say it won't hold until they pay *Pachamama* (earth goddess).

Roscoe knew about *Pachamama* and the Aymara's custom of appeasing her. "How will they do it?" he asked. "They'll have to offer a sacrifice," the muleteer answered nonchalantly.

Meetings every night in the tent swept away any thought of *Pachamama*. Roscoe was deeply engrossed in planting this new church.

Many months later we drove across the new Choquechaca bridge. Roscoe remembered what the muleteer had said about offering a sacrifice to *Pachamama*, so told the story to believers riding with us.

"They hired a good engineer to build the bridge. But they also paid a young fellow to sell his father. They gave him alcohol, until he was dead drunk, then dropped him in with the piling at the end of the bridge and poured concrete over him. You see, the bridge still holds today, so they say it's because of the sacrifice to *Pachamama*." he paused for emphasis. "But the truth is, they hired a good engineer."

The brethren remained silent. Older ones in the faith nodded in agreement, but the new believers had doubts, for they feared *Pachamama*.

"As you know, animism teaches the necessity of sacrifice," Roscoe explained, glad for the opportunity to touch on delicate subjects with new believers. "As we travel on the altiplano we see blood splashed across the sides of houses for blessing or sprinkled over potato fields for a good crop. Here in the Yungas people sprinkle it in their coca fields or splash it in the mine shafts for protection. They don't know that Jesus is the last sacrifice, and He's the one who gives blessing and protection."

We always felt the urge to push on down the trail. The community of Pataloa sat at the end of its trail. After driving to the end of the road, the fellows loaded equipment onto mules, then hiked 45 minutes to a small farm of 21 families living in this tranquil, unhurried setting.

On balmy evenings light brown, fan-tailed turkeys cackled as they found their roost in kapok trees. Flocks of squawking parrots settled into *sequile* trees to be ready for a succulent meal of ripe red coffee berries next morning. Bats darted out from their secret hiding place, and it was night. The constant roar of the river far below lulled all to sleep.

Next morning all awakened to listen to tiny green tree frogs whistling their shrill song after a fast morning shower, the throaty warble of little grey doves perched low in the orange trees, the crow of the rooster and the bray of a donkey. From somewhere below in the trees wafted a thin ribbon of smoke and the aroma of coffee.

God's orchestration of nature set the tone for the meetings. Seventeen families responded to His call. Seventeen entire families! Thrilled, we thanked the Lord.

As we came back to disciple believers, dedicate babies and encourage, we found a young fellow from the logging camp directing meeting. He led the singing while happily playing the only musical instruments, a bass and a snare drum. Excitement ran high and the church grew.

Alas, another denomination came into that small community, and took half the group to start another church. Their leader didn't stay long and left a handful of believers with no shepherd.

We were sad. But even in the face of a few discouraging moments, we saw the Lord working. Churches grew and there were open doors for tent meetings because the brethren evangelized their neighbors. More students came to Bible School than we could easily handle. It was an encouraging and exciting time! Could it be that we were beginning to see the answer to our prayer for 1000 souls? Could it be that we didn't reckon with God's timing?

The Yungas Quarterly Meeting met in Yarija in 1961.

Public transportation had gone on strike because of economic problems within the government. We thought there would be a small crowd, but more than 200 brethren walked from all corners of the field. The pastor from Caranavi, eight hours away by truck, got there in time for the last service. He had walked. Believers came from hours away on foot. One woman from Chimani walked parts of two days—up over the mountain pass and down again. A daughter guided her old blind father three days over the trail. Believers came from North Yungas, South Yungas, Caranavi, from above the mountain pass and from the interior—hours of walking!

Since the Yarija church would only seat about 75 people, we met outside. During the day we met in the shade of orange trees. At night the stars provided a dome overhead as we listened to the Word. The white walls of the church provided the large screen for showing pictures of Palestine. Showers of blessings fell—a revival for all.

They dropped their Bolivianos into the offering basket to support the Caranavi work and felt a great satisfaction knowing they were supporting missionary work.

"Pastor, here is money for tracts and medicine." Atanacio handed Roscoe a generous offering of $45.00.

We saw Yungas believers accepting the challenge of supporting their own work. God was answering prayer.

In the midst of all the excitement of growth and outreach, a letter arrived from the States. In essence it read:

> "....the mission board feels the Lord would have you move to Peru to take up that work when Cammacks come home...."

It hit us like a bomb-shell! The entire family rebelled!

"NO, we aren't going!" the children cried.

"I don't want to leave our warm climate," one complained. "It's cold up there."

"There are no trees—no place to hunt," Gary grumbled.

"There's no swimming pool."

"And no playhouse."

Everyone talked at once; but it was Roscoe who remembered practical issues.

"No. That would mean leaving 30 churches who need our help, and a wide open door for evangelism. No, I don't want to go either."

"I'm afraid to go back up to the altitude to live. It's too high," I complained.

"We can't take our car across the border. Neither can we get our money out of it if we sell it here." Roscoe sat deep in thought. "Also it will mean starting all over as far as churches are concerned, and there will be no national church to tie to. That will make the work much harder."

"I've never known you to shun work because it was hard, but you are right, there will be no church family. The hardest thing for me will be leaving our believers. They are family." I wiped away the tears.

"Most of the missionaries are not very brave on these roads so it won't be easy to find someone to take our place." There was a long silence. "And the truth is that whoever comes here has to have a burden for the people; otherwise, it will be just plain hard work."

We wrote the board that we doubted the Lord's calling us to Peru but promised to pray about it.

We searched the Scriptures while praying hard and long. "Lord, close the door if this isn't of you. Show us your way." And we reminded Him of His promise, "As ye go, the way will open up before you step by step."

Several weeks later, while going about our daily tasks, we began hearing bits of "kid talk".

"When we get to Peru, we can go fishing in the lake."

"When we get to Peru I hope we have a bigger bedroom."

"When we get to Peru, Daddy, will you help me build my go-cart?"

Without our pushing the issue, they began to change. God was working in their hearts.

Then one morning Roscoe came down to announce, "Listen to what God says this morning from Deuteronomy. 'Ye have dwelt long enough in this mount; turn ye and get ye up to the high plains.' Does that sound like God's orders for us?"

I was stunned. I didn't want to go but here God was speaking to our situation. We read on, discovering promises, which we marked in red.

I was afraid of living in the altitude again. God said, "As thy day, so shall thy strength be."

"The work will be difficult. They don't accept the Gospel easily over there," Roscoe said.

Again God said, "As I was with Moses, so I will be with thee: I will not fail thee nor forsake thee. Be strong and of good courage; be not afraid, neither be thou dismayed; for the Lord thy God is with thee, whithersoever thou goest."

"God is showing us the way so how can we stay here?" Roscoe argued as we discussed His leading. We've sown the Seed and someone else will water and harvest. But it's God's church and it will remain after we are gone. When He says *go*, we'd better go."

We stood on the veranda that evening. A full moon crept over the mountain to the east, casting long shadows across the canyon. The raucous sound of the cicada mixed with fireflies blinking through the flowers. Tears wet our cheeks as we realized we would no longer listen to these sounds or enjoy the beauty of the tropical night. Walking out to the edge of the pool Roscoe reached up to pick a red hibiscus and tucked it in my hair; then he wiped away my tears.

We bade good-bye to the Yungas brethren to the strains of "God Be With You Till We Meet Again." Following the narrow ribbon of road up the shadowy canyon, we feasted on the beauty as though we feared it would be our last time to see it—tall, spindly *kayaco* trees with clusters of huge umbrella leaves at the top, leaning out over the road at a 30-degree angle to catch the light; wild *lluvia de oro*, orange flame vine, climbing through the undergrowth; *uchi* nests swinging out into space from *sequile* trees; giant vines vying for space with the huge climbing split-leaf philodendron; pink begonias and tiny red fuchias. All seemed to wave as we passed.

Along the raging Unduavi River, past white, foamy waterfalls, we ducked behind "Old Faithful" mountain; then, skirting craggy mountains and white glaciers, we left the shadows behind as we climbed through fog drifting over icy peaks, finally breaking through into the light of a clear, deep blue sky as we wound up the last bit of zigzag road over the Andean pass.

Stopping at the top we reminisced about the six years we had spent in the Yungas. Realizing there were few level spots, everything was either "up" or "down" in that area, we prayed that the Aymara believers would keep climbing in their walk with the Lord. We felt at peace about leaving, knowing that behind every fold of purple mountains were Aymaras who would carry the Gospel on down the canyons, across the next ridge, around the bend of the river and follow winding roads on and on to the end of the trail, and beyond......

The end of the trail - (homesteaders)

Epilogue—Still Climbing

Twenty years later we went back to see what had happened to the Seed we had planted in the Yungas. We were amazed and thrilled to see how God was building His church. What did we see? We saw God performing miracles.

When we made a trip to the Yungas the whole country of Bolivia was in the midst of a transportation strike. Gas pumps were closed, but we had enough gas to start our trip and trusted God would provide along the way. He did provide: from a private mechanic in Chulumani, a few gallons from hoarding vendors in Coripata, and from a couple of barrels along the roadside where we siphoned with a hose.

"We have almost a full tank of gas," Roscoe remarked early one morning as we left Caranavi for the Alto Beni area. "We'll drive until our gauge shows half full, then we'll turn around and come back."

Our faith was small, for Alto Lima, Dos Positos and other churches on that side of the river were off the main road.

I was fearful we'd be stranded in that isolated area. "Trucks come in here only once a week so we won't find any gas for sale out here."

But the Lord always has surprises along the way. The night we finished the service at Copacabana, Carmelo followed us to the camper.

"Pastor, do you have any Aymara Bibles?"

After examining one and asking the price, he handed it back and commented wistfully, "I don't have any money now."

"Come back in the morning and we'll see what we can do." Roscoe knew Carmelo was a new believer and probably wouldn't soon have another opportunity to buy a Bible.

We watched him load two sleeping children into a wheelbarrow, then followed by his wife, they trundled off up the mountain trail.

At the peek of dawn, amid a cacophany of sounds—roosters crowing, dogs barking, a donkey braying, and turkeys, uchis and parrots taking flight from their roosts, we heard a light tap on our camnper door. We opened it to find Carmelo.

"*Buenos días*, pastor. I've come back. You see, last night I happened to think of my chain saw. I don't use it much anymore and I have this five-gallon can of gasoline that I don't need." Carmelo hesitated, not knowing quite how to barter with the missionary. "Do you—would you take this gas in exchange for a Bible? Maybe a hymnbook too," he added quickly.

Carmelo happily climbed the trail with two books and an empty gas can, while, amazed at God's provision, we sped on down the road to our next meeting.

Several days and meetings later we arrived back in Caranavi to find the filling station in operation. We pulled in for a fill-up.

"*Señor*, you don't have a drop of gas in your tank," the surprised attendant exclaimed. "You came in on fumes!"

With astonishment we listened to what sounded like gas   falling into an empty tin can. God had stretched our gasoline so we could see what He'd been doing in His church.

We spent several weeks traveling the Yungas and Caranavi areas, living in the mission camper, attending meetings in the churches and visiting with brethren in their homes.

Out of the shadows of spiritual blindness, superstition and fear, we saw many changed lives emerge. We saw mother churches encouraging new daughter churches. Once-weak congregations now thrived and were growing. Believers filled new church buildings. We found some of these new groups at the end of the roads. We would leave the camper and walk up a mountain, along a river or follow a muddy trail.

We saw second-generation believers leading services. Some older leaders had gone on to Heaven, but many were still faithful in the church. We missed some who had been deceived by cults. Then of course, some had turned from the Lord and gone back to their former animistic practices.

We saw the results of Seed that had lain dormant for several years. "Were you converted here in Llojeta?" I inquired of one young fellow after a service. "Is this your home?"

"No, I'm from Chulumani. When you brought the tent for meetings many years ago, I listened but wasn't interested. After moving here to work, one evening I heard singing—'Leaning On The Everlasting Arms'. It reminded me of that tent meeting. I came up to listen and found Jesus as my Savior."

"How wonderful!" I exclaimed. "We thought there hadn't been one convert from that meeting in Chulumani. It's true, 'His Word will not return unto Him void'."

At every service we encouraged brethren to stay true to the end. This resulted in altar services followed by long testimonies.

Mariano pleaded with us to come back to his end-of-the-road community. "If we just had one visit a year we could survive."

"I couldn't read," María testified, "but you encouraged me, and God has taught me to read. Now I can read my Bible."

"I was the heckler at the tent meeting you had here in Huayrapata," Maximo Llanqui confessed, "but I could never forget what I heard."

We also saw commitment. Salustiano spoke for the entire church as he reminisced of times of persecution, of slow growth, but of God's faithfulness. Then speaking directly to us he added, "We'll be in Heaven because you came."

His words touched our hearts. We were thankful to have played a part in the story of the Yungas, but we also reminded ourselves that God doesn't share His glory with another. It's His church. Along with these miracles of grace, we saw growth. As we drove up the mountain, leaving the Yungas behind, we reminisced. "Do you remember when we asked God for 1000 souls, 20 congregations and 10 church buildings?"

"Uh-huh," I responded. "It all proves that God's timing isn't man's timing."

"Yes, we were disappointed that he didn't answer our prayer at the time. But He really did answer; only He did it His way. There are now more than 60 churches and many more than 1000 believers. The Lord has done 'abundantly above' what we asked or thought."

I nodded, and as we passed the castle I imagined I saw a bright red hibiscus waving good-bye.

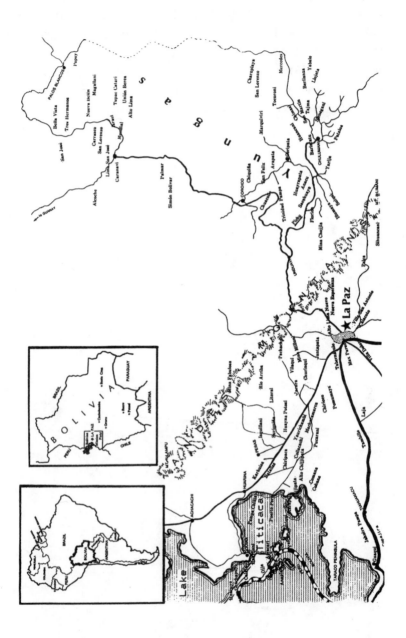

GLOSSARY

Ahuayo (ah-WAH-yo)..........Large square of colorful
cloth used by Aymara
women for carrying things
on their backs
Altiplano (ahl-tee-PLAH-no)...High plains of the Andes
Aymara (aye-MAH-rah)......Large Indian tribe of the
Andes
Balsa (BAHL-sah)................Reed boat of Lake
Titicaca
Bulto (BOOL-to)..................Pack carried on the back
Caballero (cah-bahl-YAIR-o)...Gentleman
Chala (CHAH-lah)..............Fibrous layers from the
stalk of the banana plant
Chuño (CHOON-yo)..........Dehydrated freeze-dried
potato
Coca (COH-cah)................Narcotic plant native to the
Yungas from which co-
caine is extracted

Don   (dohn)..............................Mister, but used only
with first name, show
ing respect or position
Gringo (GREEN-go)....................White man
Hacienda (ah-see-EN-dah)...........Large farm
Hasta luego (AHS-ta loo-A-go).....Good-bye
Hermana (air-MAH-nah).........Sister
Hermano   (air-MAH-no)...........Brother
Mantel (mahn-TEL)....................Large square cloth used
by men for carrying
things on their backs
MK...Missionary child (kid)
Peón   (pay-OWN)......................Serf, common laborer
Pichu (PEE-choo)......................Rural community in the
Yungas where Knights
lived
Quechua (KAYCH-wah)............Large Indian tribe of
the Andes, descendents
of the Incas
Raúl   (Rah-OOL)......................Roscoe's spanish name
Salteña (sahl-TANE-yah)...........Small meat pie
Sari   (SAH-ree)...........................Large rodent of the
tropics
Tata   (TAH-tah)..........................Aymara for father or
man
Uchi   (OO-chee).........................Large bird of the oriole
family
Waicani (wy-CAH-nee)............Knight's home in Pichu
Yatiri (yah-TEE-ree)...................Witchdoctor
Yuca   (YOO-cah).......................Manioc, a tropical plant
with edible, starchy
roots